EDUCATION IN EGYPT

EDUCATION IN EGYPT

Judith Cochran

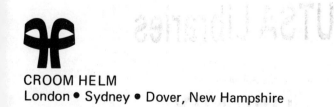

CROOM HELM
London • Sydney • Dover, New Hampshire

© 1986 Judith Cochran
Croom Helm Ltd, Provident House, Burrell Row,
Beckenham, Kent BR3 1AT
Croom Helm Australia Pty Ltd, Suite 4, 6th Floor,
64-76 Kippax Street, Surry Hills, NSW 2010, Australia

British Library Cataloguing in Publication Data

Cochran, Judith
    Education in Egypt.
    1. Education – Egypt – History
    I. Title
    370'.962   LA1646
    ISBN 0-7099-3447-5

Croom Helm, 51 Washington Street, Dover,
New Hampshire 03820, USA

Library of Congress Cataloging in Publication Data

Cochran, Judith
    Education in Egypt.

    Includes index.
    1. Education–Egypt–history. 2. Education–economic
aspects–Egypt. I. Title.
LA1646.C63   1986   370'.962   85-28017
ISBN 0-7099-3447-5

Printed and bound in Great Britain by
Biddles Ltd, Guildford and King's Lynn

CONTENTS

List of Tables
Preface
Introduction

Tables

For my parents
Joseph and Dorothy Cochran

Preface

I arrived in Cairo in September of 1980 as the first Fulbright senior lecturer in education in over 15 years. I soon found myself involved in much more than teaching educational psychology and curriculum development on the graduate and undergraduate level at Ain Shams University. The Dean of the College of Education, Abdul Gaffar Abdul Salam, was also chairman of a national subcommittee in charge of assessing the competencies of 140,000 primary school teachers in Egypt, 139,000 of which were not certified. This assessment was part of the Ministry of Education's total reorganization plan which involved the restructuring of primary and secondary education. During 1980-81 school year, Dr. William Ebied, Dr. Mohammed Mofti and I developed a competency based observation instrument which was used by graduate students who visited the elementary classrooms in the twelve educational zones of Cairo. This observation system was expanded the following year to involve over sixty university professors throughout the country in addition to the original group of professors and graduate students who had conducted the Cairo study.

In order to continue participating in the primary teacher assessment, I accepted the directorship of the DPS English language program at American University in Cairo. Here, I worked with over 150 part-time teachers and 8,000 students, most of which were Egyptian. The English instructors taught in local elementary and secondary schools, worked as inspectors, school directors, college professors, Ministry of Education officials and then came to A.U.C. as a second or third job. As the director of a large educational program at American University in Cairo and member of the team of Egyptian educators conducting research for Dean Abdul Gaffar who soon became the Egyptian Minister of Education, I was in an advantageous position to participate, observe and research Egyptian education. But I had no intentions of writing this book.

It wasn't until I began meeting confused foreign investors and consultants that I began to understand the wealth of information and resources available to me. The book had to be written to increase the educational understanding of Egyptians and international investors. So at night, during the weekends and over vacations, I had began to research the puzzle that I had found. As the educational leader in the Middle East, education received in Egypt and mostly in Cairo shaped present and future social, economic and religious movements in the area. This educational system with its enormous influence was difficult to understand, neglected by foreign scholars and comprehended by Egyptians. I had begun making observational notes as I went to elementary and secondary schools throughout Egypt. When I showed these notes to the director of the National Center for Educational Research, he informed me that I needed to read more about Egyptian education. As he brought books to my office, I began to learn the complexities of integrating resources in Arabic, French, English, existing mostly in private collections. After I checked out the four books on Egyptian education available at A.U.C. library, I began to ask my friends for books and articles on education in Egypt. Friends on the Supreme Council of Universities brought me reports they and their students had written, Ministry of Education officials gave their valuable time for interviews and supplied me with official reports, many of which had not been translated. The reports from the President's Council, the equivalent of a Presidential Advisory Board, were the gift of their friends who understood the importance of having relevant, accurate documentation. And once I began to put the resources together, they didn't agree.

Inconsistencies in the documentation became the basis for the further investigation which lead me to USAID and World Bank references. I had known participants on many of the USAID projects as they had either been a part of the international community, come to A.U.C., or contacted me through the Fulbright office. Through Dean Abdul Gaffar Abdul Salam, I had met the director of World Bank projects in Middle East, Europe, Far East and Asia. With his aid, I visited World Bank project sites, talked to participants and documented the development of World Bank projects. And I checked and re-checkedmy information with teachers, the Egyptian leaders of the Ministry of Education, students, fellow Fulbrighters, USAID officials, and visiting consultants. The list of those who aided me must include all of the teachers in the A.U.C. English language program, most especially the group which called themselves the "old hands," fellow professors at Ain Shams, Tanta, Minya, Assuit, and Cairo universities, Dr. Youssif Khalil and Dr. Salah

Kotb, both eminent and respected members of the President's Council and Supreme Council of Universities, and friends like Dr. Gammal Abdul Nasser, Mohammed Hassen, Dr. Carl and Judy Mills, Dr. Frank and Betty Blanning. Dr. Arthur Goldschmidt, Jr., a Fulbright scholar and Middle East historian who along with Dr. Salah Kotb, and Dr. Charles Clark, spent many hours reading the manuscript and making suggestions about style and content. In final analysis, this work is to aid those who come to Egypt and the Middle East to study and work among her people. More than this, it is a testimony to the kindness and dedication of men and women like George Dawood, Ramsey Kamel, Latif Doss, Guirgis Rashidi, and Reda Salama who have provided leadership for over forty years in Egyptian schools. I hope this book reveals their concerns, accomplishments, and friendship. This is, after all, their story.

CENTURY OF CONFLICT

EDUCATION IN CONTEMPORARY EGYPT

Introduction

Education is a critical force in contemporary Egyptian development. Egyptian education is the past and present architect of economic and social behavior in the Middle East and throughout the Muslim world. For over a thousand years, Al-Azhar University has been the center of Islamic scholarship, education, and thought. Muslims educated at Al-Azhar have extended Egypt's influence far beyond her borders. And early in the nineteenth century, Egypt forged ahead of the rest of the Muslim world in secular education, after Mohammed Ali set up the first modern medical, veterinary, engineering, and accounting schools in the area. During British colonial rule of Egypt, state-controlled education was structured to serve British interests while Egyptians and non-English foreigners worked to expand private and religious education. Following Britain's declaration of Egyptian independence in 1922, great advances took place in public education at all levels. Egypt's educational leadership expanded even more during the presidency of Gamal Abdel Nasser, who offered free secular and religious education, through the doctorate, for Egyptians and students from other Muslim countries. While importing students, Egypt exported teachers and administrators to the rest of the Arab world. They set up and staffed schools and universities on so large a scale that Egyptians can claim to have shaped the secular and religious leadership of most of the Arab countries. Today Egypt's educational system both reflects and augments the social unrest of its own people--and of those it has influenced. Historic conflicts between religious and secular leaders, between tradition and innovation, and between foreign and national interests, influence contemporary Egyptian education. And the education of her youth has and will set the course for Egypt's future economic and social development.

CHAPTER I

ROOTS OF MODERN EDUCATION

For the 5,000 years of recorded history and no
doubt before, Egyptian civilization revolved around
the Nile. Its waterway provided irrigation for
nearby farms and transportation of produce to
markets. Survival needs educated Egyptians about the
Nile, farming and the sale of goods. And this
knowledge, passed from father to son, enabled
Egyptians to be secure and thrive in a country which
was an agricultural and commerical center for
thousands of years. But her geographic accessibility
and natural resources also made Egypt a desirable
acquisition. In ancient history, she was a part of
the Hyksos, Assyrian, Persian, and Macedonian
Empires. As a part of the Roman Empire, Christian
Egyptians were persecuted and fled to the desert and
Upper Egypt where they continued their farming and
religion far from the commerical and agricultural
centers. As an urban civilization flourished on the
banks of the Nile, Egyptians developed such skills
as writing, geometry, surveying, accounting, human
and veterinary medicine, and administration. The
formal education that existed took place in the
temples. Thus, from earliest times, education and
religion were inseparable. And while they may have
been taxed and persecuted, most Egyptians did not
find their lives or educational needs greatly
altered regardless of the different ruling Empires.
The foreign rulers continued as a society unto
themselves, interested in the resources of the
country but not the culture nor the people.
After several centuries under the Byzantine
(East Roman) Empire, Egypt fell in 642 to Muslim
troops from Arabia. In order to convert the
Egyptians to Islam, mosques were begun in every
village. Each mosque had a school, or Kuttab, where

young Egyptian boys were taught to read and write in order to learn the teachings of Islam, revealed to the Prophet Mohammad in the Koran. Thus, Arabic, the language of the Koran, became the language of the people and Islam became the religion of most Egyptians. Then the Arab caliphate power declined and between 868 and 969 two Turkish dynasties governed Egypt. In 969, the Turks were overcome by another Islamic dynasty, the Fatimids from North Africa. They founded a capital named Cairo and established the University of Al-Azhar, a major center of Islamic learning. Here, exceptional Kuttab students could further their knowledge of Islam and become the most highly educated Egyptians. During the 1160's the Fatimid caliph called upon Syria to supply troops for wars against the Christian crusaders. This action enabled Saladin, a successful Syrian officer, to take control of Egypt. The Ayyubid dynasty, founded by Saladin, ruled Egypt from 1171 to 1250.

In order to maintain military control of the country, the Fatimid and Ayyubid dynasties bought boy slaves from Circassia and Turkish Central Asia. These youths were educated in special schools where they were taught the Islamic faith, loyalty to the foreign rulers, methods of administration and warfare. Called Mameluks, warriors could marry Egyptian women, but their children could not be educated as Mameluks. The Ayyubid dynasty was overthrown by the Mamleluks, who proceeded to expand their power into Syria, Paurtine, and Western Arabia. The Mamleluks were trusted more than the Egyptians, and the Ottoman rulers gave them authority to rule the land, collect taxes from Egyptians and report to the Ottoman governor. The Mameluks organized cavalry squadrons and resisted Napoleon I when he invaded Egypt in 1798. After the French defeated the Mameluks in the Battle of the Pyramids, some joined the French army while others remained with the Ottomans to drive the French out of Egypt in 1801. After four years of conflict, Mehemet or Mohammed Ali, a Turkish soldier from Albania, seized control of the country. He drove out a British force occupying Alexandria and in 1811, massacred the remaining Mameluks leaders at a banquet in Cairo. Mohammed Ali now controlled Egyptian economic and military resources.

Since the Arab invasion 300 years earlier, there had been no significant change in the agrarian life of the Egyptian. Now Mohammed Ali introduced cotton and hemp farming. Irrigation was expanded

3

and a barrage or dam on the Nile was begun. Mohammed Ali nationalized and later redistributed the land thus creating a middle class of wealthy Turks though his encouragement of agricultural development. Mohammed Ali was most interested in building a modern army and navy to support his wars of conquest in Arabia, Greece, the Sudan and Syria. But he could not import enough foreign experts to increase and up-grade his armed forces, which depended on modern technology and weaponry. He needed, therefore, to train Egyptians.

Unfortunately, the Egyptian's religious education and agrarian background did not prepare them to comprehend technical military and secular curriculum. So Mohammed Ali sent missions of bright young Egyptians abroad to be educated. He also founded high schools to produce infantry, cavalry and artillery officers. Soon his army needed doctors, engineers, pharmacists, veterinarians and technicians capable of building and repairing weapons. He also needed an administrative structure loyal to him. To meet this demand, he established a school of accounting (1826) an engineering school (1829) and a school for administration (1834). (Szyliowicz, 1973, p.103) Because this emergent higher education had been established before primary and secondary schools, he was forced to use the existing religious education network as the source of students. Mohammed Ali thus found it necessary to add a system of public secondary and primary schools. By beginning with higher education and ending with elementary education, he implemented what has been called a reversed educational pyramid system. (Farag, 1976, p.43).

By the time of his death in 1849, Mohammed Ali had created a significant change in the Egyptian's life; he had educated an Egyptian middle class which was a source of rebellion for his heirs. Abbas, Mohammed Ali's successor, closed most of the secondary technical schools and Said, who followed Abbas, contributed to the decline of "modern" secular education by closing even more. A stagnation period for Egyptian education began which continued through the end of Said's rule in 1863. This is not to say that the foreigners did not have their own elite schools; most of these schools were set up after the reign of Said. Each had their own educational system which was conducted in their language and directed loyalties of students toward the "mother" country. After the reign of Said, French, British, German and American missionary schools were added to the "ecoles libres gratuites et universelles," and schools for the Greek, Italian, Jewish and Armenian minorities also were added. Also several primary and secondary schools were founded by the Egyptian Christians (Copts), particularly the Coptic secondary school in Cairo, the Narcossia school in Alexandria and several other secondary schools in the governorates which were owned and run by Coptic notables and societies. All of these "foreign language" schools admitted and educated some Egyptians with the Copt schools solely educating young Egyptians.

While Mohammed Ali's secular schools were in decline these "language" or foreign schools greatly increased in number from 1840 onward. Foreign schools received financial support from the Ottoman governors, especially Ismail Pasha, Said's successor, who aimed to create a foreign educational system to complement his "westernization" of Egypt. The Riad program of 1874 was an attempt by Egyptians to place foreign schools under the control of the government. However, it was not put into effect, as it was not approved by the legislature. (Harby, 1960, p.46).

The growth of the foreign schools and their successful education of an Egyptian elite caused Gamel El Din El Afghani and his student Mohammad Abduh to address the educational needs of the Egyptian masses. The resulting Law of 19 Rajab 1284 (1867) provided for the total reorganization of education and recognized the necessity of spreading education among the people. Kuttab corrections and developments were implemented under the name of "domestic schools" to be integrated with surviving technical schools begun by Mohammed Ali. However, this law too was never fully implemented. (Harby, 1960,p.47). Education was not Ismail's only concern as he continued to "westernize" Egypt. He rebuilt parts of Cairo as a replica of Paris, and while the building of the Suez Canal was a co-operativeeffort between the French and Egyptians, a company administered by the French was allowed to operate the canal for 99 years. In 1875, Egypt's financial condition worsened. In 1876, the government appointed two British and French officials to manage its financial affairs. In 1881, Egyptians, many of whom had been educated abroad under Mohammed Ali and his successors, revolted against control by the Turkish rulers and the British and French advisors. After Egyptian riots broke out in Alexandria in 1882, British troops put down the revolt and occupied Egypt maintaining the Ottoman khedive or king as puppet ruler.

Throughout history, Egyptian education had reflected the dichotomy of its society. Egypt had been ruled for centuries by a succession of foreigners educated in their own schools with loyalties to their "mother" countries. These ruling classes had little contact with the average Egyptian who, if educated, had attended Coptic or Islamic religious schools (kuttabs). A few educated Egyptians held religious ranks and represented the people to the rulers. A small group of secularly educated middle-class Egyptians had emerged from Mohammed Ali's educational system. But his intent had never been to educate the masses. As he wrote in a letter to his son, Ibrahim, "What Europe is suffering from is the result of generalizing the education among all levels of society so they're involved...they have no chance of avoiding what happened. So if this is an example in front of us, so our duty is to just teach them how to read and write to a certain limit in order to accomplish satisfied work and not to spread education beyond this point." (Moursi, 1974,p.12). Therefore, the majority of Egyptians were poor laborers without political and social power.

Two separate but equal elite educational systems had emerged--one for technological, practical, specialized training and the other for spiritual, cultural instruction. The masses continued to receive elementary religious education in the kuttabs. But the intellectual Egyptians were to be divided between those who had graduated from Al-Azhar and those who were products of Mohammed Ali's new technical institutions. In this manner, an institutional cleavage arose with fateful consequences for Egypt's future development. An elite-masses gap was perpetuated. Furthermore, the elite were to be divided between those having secular and religious education. (Doss, 1983, interview).

The secular elite had been trained in skills useful for professional and commercial endeavors of the present and the future while the religious elite had been trained in skills useful for interpreting the social and religious mandates of the past. The demonstrated expertise of foreign technicians and invaders had forced Egyptians into a cultural conflict. If Egypt was to develop economically and maintain itself as a commercial and agricultural center, both systems had to be integrated to provide an appropriate education for all Egyptians.

But life for all Egyptians had changed. The Suez Canal and later the Aswan Dam (both on the Nile) reduced the significance of the Nile as the center of life for the Egyptian. Its water, polluted and carrying the debilitating belharzia, (a disease caused by snails) could not irrigate enough land to feed its population. While its waterways remained a source of transportation for a few, roads became the competitor as trucks, buses and carts carried far more produce to market. Technicians were needed to improve agricultural methods, develop transportation systems for a rapidly expanding population and move Egypt competitively into whatever high technology developments the future demanded. However, Egyptian emphasis upon technology and its concomitant commercial and economic leadership threatened religious leadership of the past providing Egyptians with either ambiguous choices for the future or obedience to the past. The problems facing Egypt, the challenging ones needing urgent attention, have become those of social change and modification to enable the agrarian Egyptian to adapt to and use the technology that arrives with and forms the basis of economic development. But such changes also involve a change of social values, skills and institutions which have operated successfully for thousands of years. The task of Egyptian education in the twentieth century has been to integrate two seemingly incompatible value systems; one secular and foreign, the other religious and Egyptian. The resolution of this conflict has been the history of education in Egypt for the past century and promises to dictate the future for years to come.

CHAPTER I REFERENCES

Boktor, Amir. (1963). "The Development and Expansion of Education in the United Arab Republic," American University in Cairo Press, Cairo, ARE.

Doss, Latif, retired official, Ministry of Education. Personal Interview.

Farag, Alya. (1976). "The Education in Egypt Between Local and Government Efforts," El Marrif Organization, Cairo, ARE.

Harby, Mohammed. (1960). "Education in the United Arab Republic in the Twentieth Century," General Organization for Gobernment Printing, Cairo, ARE.

Hyde, Georgie D. M. (1973). "Education in Modern Egypt, Ideals and Realities," London, England. Routledge and Kegan Paul.

Iskandar, H. (1972). "Problems of Bilingual Education in English Schools in Egypt." TEFL paper. Washington, D.C.

Moursi, M. M. (1974). "The World of Writing," The Higher Education Department.

Naser, Famal Abdel. (1954). "Philosophy of Revolution," Cairo, U.A.R.

Rizk, Nazli Hanna: (1981). "Factors Affecting the Standard of Achievement in English of Student in English Language Schools in Egypt," unpublished master's thesis, American University in Cairo, Cairo.

Samaan, Sadek. (1955). "Value Reconstruction and Egyptian Education," Columbia University Press, New York, New York.

Stephens, Robert Henry. (1972). "Nasser: A Political Biography," Simon and Shuster, New York, New York.

Szyliowicz, Joseph. (1973). "Education and Modernization in the Middle East," Cornell University Press, London, England.

CHAPTER II

BRITISH OCCUPATION, 1882-1919

The Egyptian government was almost bankrupt by 1876. Ismail Pasha was forced to appoint a European commission to supervise the collection of state revenues and the repayment of government debts. Two years later he even introduced English and French ministers into his cabinet. Pressed to settle with its European creditors, the Egyptian government put off paying its own officials and military officers, driving many into dire poverty. Some rebelled. The Western powers persuaded the Ottoman sultan to dismiss Ismail in favor of his son, Tawfiq, in 1879, but Egypt's economic problems persisted. A group of Egyptian officers and civil servants, many of them trained in government schools founded by Mohammed Ali or Ismail, rebelled against their privileged Turkish overlords and their European advisors. They gained the backing of nearly all classes of Egypt's society, took control of the government, and instituted constitutional reforms. After riots broke out in Alexandria in 1882, British troops entered the country to suppress the rebellion. While promising to leave as soon as order had been restored to Egypt, the British established a military occupation that was to last for 74 years. Westernizing reform thus led to Western rule.

In 1882, the British army and the British agent and counsel general became the actual governing forces behind the Turkish khedive, who remained as the titular head of Egypt. The British, like previous occupying powers, created a separate economic and social stratum for themselves which revolved around the exclusive Alexandria and Cairo Sporting Clubs. There, British officers and soldiers could enjoy horse-racing, golf, swimming, tennis, squash and dining facilities. And once more, there was little effort on the part of foreign rulers to improve or alter the educational or economic life of most Egyptians.

In 1883, when Sir Evelyn Baring began his 20-year service as British agent and counsel general, the educational system had operated for more than 30 years with little government interference. Mandatory literacy had been decreed in 1867 requiring that within 18 years all members of the legislative council should be able to read and write and members of the electorate should achieve literacy within 30 years. The decree was abandoned in 1888 because of the lack of personnel to staff the schools. Proposals to reform education were made in 1867 and 1880 but not put into effect because of the political conflicts of those periods. In 1883, the elite secular education consisted of 270 primary schools and three specialized secondary schools, remnants of Mohammed Ali's technical educational system. In addition, there were 60 students in an Arabic teacher training school at Dar Al Ulum, 300 girls in female schools, and 48,664 students in the foreign or "language" schools. Most Egyptian males, however, were educated in the 9,647 religious kuttabs or one of the 4,664 elementary schools begun by the state at different times to provide free education for the poor. (Harby, 1960, p.4). Baring, faced with a fiscal crisis and not expecting the British occupation to last very long, slashed educational expenses. But what started as an emergency measure survived the government's financial crisis and became, in effect, Britain's educational policy in Egypt.

Facilities and curricula improvement required money, but the financial investment in education during the British occupation was minimal. The coffers of Egypt had been emptied by Mohammed Ali and the wars of Ismail Pasha. Little had been spent on education since the early 1846's. Prior to British occupation, education in kuttabs, modern technical, and elementary schools had been free. But, by 1907, free education was entirely prohibited by order of Baring. Even those educated in "modern" primary or elementary schools for the poor had to be at least middle class, while the poor Egyptians went to kuttabs which were funded at various levels by the endowment of each mosque or church. In 1889, the state budget showed a surplus of more than 200,000 pounds but still no money was invested in education. L.E.69,479 was allowed for education of which L.E.12,745 was recovered in school fees.

(Boktor, 1936, p.133). All schools which operated without government support continued to increase, indicating interest on the part of Egyptians in obtaining an education.

Foreign language and missionary schools flourished. On the other hand, the modern technical schools created by Mohammed Ali floundered with three specialized secondary schools continuing--two industrial workshops and one industrial school in Mansura. As late as 1911, all graduates of these schools were employed by the government. (Boktor, 1963, p.140). Modern technical schools still provided no cultural subjects such as history and the only requirements for admission were the ability to read and write and knowledge of simple rules of arithmetic. Both the workshops and the industrial school were self-supporting from the all of the students' products and their wages for work conducted. In 1906, the government established a department for vocational education with the object of supervising this much needed type of instruction. In 1911, an institute was begun in which commercial courses were taught at two levels, intermediate and secondary. But, until 1910, there was only one agricultural school in a largely agrarian country. A primary education certificate was required for admisssion, which meant that the candidates for the agricultural school came from the same applicant pool as those for secondary schools. Because the latter provided a better education, students often chose secondary schools, thus limiting the expansion of the agricultural school. (Harby, 1960, p.10).

Similarly, the vocational schools for women continued but were not encouraged financially by the British. The first foreign school for girls was opened by an American mission in 1856, followed in 1873 by the first Egyptian school for girls, founded by Tcheshme-Afet, third wife of Ismail Pasha. Only the very privileged girls had any educational opportunities at all; some Christian girls went to European or Missionary schools. In 1910, a vocational school for women was set up at Kobri El Koubra, providing specialized study of home economics, embroidery, and needlework. (Boktor, 1963,p.142). Admission to this school required the post-elementary education certificate, but the curriculum revealed little interest in educating women for occupations outside the home. The growth of schools for women was limited partially by the lack of teachers. It was extremely difficult, if not impossible, to find native women teachers.

11

Apart from the fact that very few women were educated, it was considered shameful for a woman to earn a living and even more shameful to earn a living by teaching. Thus, Egyptian schools were forced to obtain their female teachers from Europe and from other Arabic-speaking countries, notably Syria. (Boktor, 1963, p.144). In the few government schools begun for girls, a male teacher was always accompanied in class by a European woman whose sole duty was to chaperon girls. The chief reason for few facilities for female education was the limited need for educated females. Government school enrollment and graduation were controlled by examinations which were no longer developed by the teachers but constructed by a British Board of Examiners. The questions were written by the board, and the answers were taken to the British Advisor himself to be submitted to the examiners for grading. In 1898 of the 1,381 candidates examined for the primary education certificate, only 427 passed. (Harby, 1960, p.14).

Furthermore, the goverment schools did not encourage independent thinking, as memorization was the means of preparing for the Civil Service exam.

> I understand that little is known about educational psychology and memorizing is the normal practice. In one school, I heard that a syllabus is prepared, and if a student successfully memorizes it he can pass the examinations of the school and the Civil Service without recourse to a single book. (Harris, 1925, p.69).

Courses in the government schools were influenced by the fact that there were very few job opportunities outside of the Civil Service and selection was based upon examination scores. The secondary education certificate examination was also a reflection of governmental need. From 1887 to 1890, there was a relaxation of examination standards, as there was a need for government workers. Students who failed merely took the exam the following year. (Tibawi, 1972, p.81). In 1891 only 28 out of 128 passed that examination; in 1892, only 36 passed out of 90 applicants. (Boktor, 1936, p.133). In addition to preventing students from continuing their education, the exams also controlled the number of candidates for specific government positions, a process which paralleled Mohammed Ali's procedure of training only as many technicians as were needed for his military endeavors. The difference was that, while engaged in warfare Mohammed Ali expanded the number of schools, while under British rule, numbers were restricted through examinations, fees, and a lack of facilities.

The education of religious elite continued unaltered from the 500 years of Turkish rule, during which Mameluks were trained to become Amirs (someone who gives orders) and Egyptians were trained to become Ulamas, (someone who interprets the Koran and Hadith). The British did not alter the secular and religious elitist educational system. The only difference was that the British trained the secular elite to be English speaking governmental bureaucrats rather than members of a military machine. The curriculum of elite government schools encouraged submission to authority and passiveness which limited independent thought. Some subjects which could have helped build a socially intelligent graduate were excluded from the curricula. For example, the following were not taught in any school in Egypt: ethics; economics; philosophy, ancient or modern; and Arabic and European literature. (Wilson, 1928, p.76-77) The religious and secular educational systems had become such that the less individuality and initiative shown by the Egyptian, the more acceptable he was likely to be to the advisor whose duty it was to train him for bureaucratic station. (White, 1899, p.27). This curriculum was perhaps too successful, if Mufti Shaykh Nunammad Abduh (1898) is to be believed:

> As a rule one thing alone is exacted in a candidate for a public office and that is that he should possess a nature entirely passive. A man in the smallest degree independent will not be admitted or if by mistake he should be, he will not remain long. The Egyptian officials do not tell the truth, they take no initiative, approve all that is wanted and never oppose any measure. (Stevans, 1898, p.77).

No words can express the Egyptian official's ineptitude, his laziness, his helplessness, his

13

dread of responsibilitiy, his maddening red tape formalism. His panacea in every unexpected case is the same. It must be put in writing; he must ask for instructions. (Stevans, 1898, p.116). However, according to Cooper(1913): the graduates of the religious system which culminated with Al-Azhar University were not much better.

> The college student in Egypt, if he may already be called such, is a past master at imitation. He lacks mental resourcefulness. His mind is automatic rather than creative. Students in the secondary schools, as in other grades, will point with worthy pride to their drawings which are copies of originals and their Arabic maps, which are really wonders of calligraphy and systematic imitation. Centuries of memorizing have produced a condition of brain similar to that which we find today in China, where the students have been busied with the memorizing of Confucius and other ancient books as the chief activiy of education. Even the native teachers in these schools, when asked for original opinions will fumble for their catalogues of the schedules and rules which have been laid down for that school and which for them are as authoritative as the Koran itself. This lack of personal responsibility and adaptation, produced by centuries of serfdom, seems to be an inherent weakness in Egyptian character. (Cooper, 1913 p.134).

DeGuerville also found religious education inadequate preparation for political and economic leadership.

> I asked the Muslem sheikh who accompanied me to Al-Azhar what would be the result of this learning upon the students. He replied: These men are becoming authorities upon the theology and the sacred laws of (Islam) Mohammedanism; they will be the priests and jurists of Islam;

they will go out to various towns and rural communities of Egypt, as well as to other countries, to be expounders of the Sacred Law covering all matters of daily living. But of the outside world and of the relationship of learning to modern life, these men will be as ignorant as when they entered Al-Azhar. (DeGuerville, 1905, p.161).

Recognizing the foreign influence in the education of their young, the Egyptians demanded that Arabic be the main language of teaching in primary and secondary schools, although French and English could, and did, continue as additional languages of instruction. In government schools, English or French and Arabic became compulsory subjects. In private language schools, however, French or English continued to be the principal language of instruction. Thus, the demands of the people were met, but they demanded too little. The curricula, exams, purposes of education, and number and quality of graduates were not questioned.

The same year, in 1908, a group of Egyptian notables and leaders made subscriptions and began a university. Khedive Abbas II, the Turkish king of Egypt at that time, ordered that an annual grant in aid of L.E.2,000 should be paid to the university. Moreover, his personal influence encouraged others to contribute generously to this enterprise. His son, Prince Foad, was elected president of the Egyptian University, which was officially inaugurated on a small scale in December, 1908. Fewer than 10 courses were offered to the small, transient student body. (Tignor, 1966, p. 338). Its chief function consisted of providing lectures for general culture. Orientalists were invited from the European universities to lecture on literature, philosophy, sociology and history. Other lectures on higher mathematics, astronomy and physics were in the hands of the best Egyptian lecturers available. Twenty-four students were sent to Europe to specialize in various subjects and return to lecture at the university. Prince Foad, realizing the importance of a library, used his influence in Egypt and Europe to build one.

By 1910, there seemed to be a general movement toward some educational expansion under Saad Zaghlul, the Minister of Public Education. Nine new agricultural schools were opened between 1911 and 1921. In 1911, the Giza Agricultural School was converted into a higher school and an intermediate agricultural school was founded at Moushtohor to further educate graduates of the Giza elementary schools. The following year, another intermediate agricultural school was established at Damamhur. A third school was opened at Shebin El Kom (Menufia) in 1914. (Harby, 1960, p.15).

In addition, a committee was formed to encourage students to study abroad in European colleges at their parents' expense and under the indirect control of the Egyptian Ministry of Education. In 1914, 614 students left for Europe, 372 of whom studied in Great Britain, 139 in France and 36 in Switzerland. (Newman, 1928, p.230) But once more, only the wealthy Egyptians could afford to have their children educated abroad. Clearly, government schools provided an education suited to the needs of the British.

Sir Evelyn Barings' excuse for educational deficiencies was that a quarter of a century was too short a time to effect change in the unpromising nature of the material with which the English had to work: Egypt was a country of limited possibilities, limited finances, undisciplined minds, and Turkish pashas. The English neglected education, claiming that the time had not yet come, that there was a greater need for reforms of irrigation and justice, and the abolition of corruption and graft. "It would be childish to discuss the pattern of the carpet when the house in which it was laid was on fire." (Baring, 1967, p.534). Furthermore, a uniform level of education was viewed as the only possible safeguard against the rise of nationalists who might stir the people against their foreign rulers. (Rawadan, 1951, p.535). Instead of improving the education so that people might intelligently deal with occupational forces, the British kept the general quality of education low, thus preventing the education of potentially disruptive leaders. (Baring, 1967, p.535).

The defense that can be given British policy is that they may not have had bad intentions, but rather simply allowed matters to take their slow evolutionary course. The English claimed their control of education was not direct or complete, even from the beginning of the occupation. It is quite clear, however, that the slow evolutionary course limited the number of young Egyptians who attended school. By 1913, only 6.5 percent of the girls and 20.5 percent of the boys were actually given the lowest level of education. In the same year, the number of students in schools of Egypt was 3 1/2 percent of the eligible population, compared to 15 percent in Italy and France, 16 percent in Austria, Germany and Japan, 17 percent in England and 24 percent in the U.S. (Boktor, 1936, p.146).

In 1913, a British visitor named Cooper (1913) subjectively described the difference that government funding made for elementary schools.

> I was ushered into a small room containing 20 little boys varying in ages from 7 to 10 years. The floor was covered with ragged straw matting. The decorations consisted of a blackboard, which the children sitting cross-legged on the floor were facing. A huge bottle of ink dangled from a nail on the wall. Three boys were totally blind, and exactly one half of the pupils possessed but one eye apiece. Indeed, the teacher himself, who was an utterly uneducated man, possessed but a single eye and this one so feeble and filmy that he could only discern an Arabic character by bringing the paper against his eye at a certain angle. There were no books save a few leaves from the Koran. There was no supervision from any board of education. The teacher was supported by the tuition fee of one piaster per week from each student. The school exercise was repeating together in a shrill sing-song manner certain words from one of the Surrahs of the Koran keeping time with a rhythmic swaying of their little bodies. Those words were repeated over and over again in what seemed to be an endless reiteration with the sole object of committing the words to memory, since the meaning of these theological and recondite phrases were far beyond the understanding, not only of the pupils but also of the teacher himself.

> The second elementary school received a small yearly grant from the

government and was inspected by officials from the Ministry of Education. I found here desks, some system of studies as required by the government and a general improvement in the character of the teacher. This official was also somewhat more liberally paid, receiving from each student 5 piasters a month. The school occupied a room which was originally the tomb of a Moslem sheik. The individual method of instruction was in vogue, the 20 or more students in the room were expected to study in a high voice in union with one pupil the well known words of the Koran.

The third school was entirely under government control and occupied a fine building with thorough sanitary arrangements, a room for the headmaster, with lockers for books and other modern conveniences. There were three teachers in this school receiving L.E.20.00 per month from the government in addition to a fee from 2 to 15 piasters a month from each student. This fee was exacted according to the financial ability of the boys. The torture instruments of the other "kuttabs" had disappeared and modern slates took the place of strips of tin used in other schools(19). While the British did little to improve the level of education in Egypt, many of their educational policies were culturally consistent with previous educational traditions. Limited governmental influence in traditional and private schools, little effort toward constructing schools for the masses, continuation of a curriculum which emphasized rote memory, and the secular education of a small number of elite Egyptians were policies which had been in effect from the beginning of Turkish occupation. Furthermore, British efforts were limited by financial constraints. As evidenced by the growth of private

> kuttabs and foreign language schools,
> the British did not restrict
> education when their financial
> support was not required. (p.154-
> 155).

While giving attention to what was left of
Mohammed Ali's system, the British didn't consider
the personal development of the children or societal
needs. They created an educational system mainly
available to middle or higher class students by
charging fees prohibitive to the lower-class
children. In the 40 years of British occupation,
only one exception or scholarship was awarded to an
Egyptian child and that case resulted from the
threatened resignation of Saad Zaoul, the Egyptian
Minister of Education. That scholarship student was
Ismail Cabani who became the Minister of Education
and advocate of one school for all children of
Egypt. He was granted a scholarship in 1908 for all
of his education by Lord Dunlop "on the condition
that it will never happen again." (Salah Kotb, 1983,
personal interview).

Although the financial expenditure was small,
the British gave some encouragement to the education
of women. However, the lack of a cultural tradition
to support this effort and the British policy of
only hiring men for government positions limited its
effectiveness. With a history of women's seclusion
and separation from men, co-education in government
schools was culturally incongruent. Futhermore,
having girls enroll and pay for education which
trained them for government positions available only
to men made little sense either culturally or
economically. The female schools which did succeed
were segregated and focused on learning skills such
as embroidery, needlepoint and home economics.

To summarize, Egyptian education under the
British occupation was aimed at producing obedient
clerks, not the technically or scientifically
trained leaders badly needed to develop the country.
Religious education flourished while moral and
patriotic content was lacking in the secular state
schools which were as ill-suited to Egypt's needs as
the education offered in the missionary and foreign
schools. British educational policy in Egypt was
essentially conservative, and showed little progress
beyond the reforms of Mohammed Ali and Ismail.

The British occupation of Egypt succeeded in
introducing a new focus for education--government
employment as the expected reward for the English-

speaking elite. The guarantee of a position with
the Civil Service after graduation from a government
school became firmly implanted in the people's
minds. A population of technologically,
commercially or scientifically trained leaders who
could operate the country had not been a British
aim. Thus, Baring's goal of not educating a
population which could rebel against the British was
met. Further, the neglect of religious education
served to isolate Egyptians from governmental
influence and occupational control. The British
governmental schools were congruent in philosophy
with that of the modern technical schools begun by
Mohammed Ali, and hence made no significant change
in Egyptian educational philosophy.

Until 1914, Egypt remained a privileged
province of the Ottoman Empire, but when World War
I pitted that country against the British, they
quickly deposed Khedive Abbas in favor of a more
malleable relative, declared a protectorate over
Egypt, and severed its pro forma Ottoman ties.
Although the Egyptians did not have to fight against
their Turkish overlords, their lives were affected
by the huge influence of British Empire troops, who
used their country as a base of operations against
the Ottoman Empire. Anti-British feelings grew,
culminating in a nation-wide revolution of 1919, led
by Saad Zaghlul. The British conceded independence
in 1922, but kept their troops in Egypt. From then
on they no longer tried to control Egypt's education
or other internal policies, but many British
officials, teachers and military personnel remained.
In practice, the British still influenced Egyptian
politics, which were chaotic because of the
multiplicity of political parties, royal
interference, and the lack of a clearly defined
relationship with Great Britain. Even the Anglo-
Egyptian Treaty of 1936, which called for the
withdrawal of British troops from all parts of Egypt
except the Suez Canal Zone, did not bring about the
complete independence that the nationalists had been
demanding since 1919.

CHAPTER II REFERENCES

Baring, Evelyn. (1967) "Modern Egypt," London, England. Vol. II.

Boktor, Amir. (1936) "School and Society in the Valley of the Nile," Cairo, U.A.R. Elias Modern Press.

Cooper, Clayton Sedwick. (1913) "The Man of Egypt," New York and London. Hodder and Stoughton.

De Guerville, A. B. (1905) "New Egypt, "London, England. William Heinemann.

Harby, Mohammed. (1960) "Education in United Arab Republic in the Twentieth Century," Cairo, U.A.R. General Organization for Government Printing.

Harris, Murry. (1925) "Egypt: Under the Egyptians," London, England. Chapman and Hall.

Mufti, Shaykh Muhammed Adbul in Stevans "Egypt in 1898," New York, New York. Dodd, Mead, and Co.

Newman, E. W. Polson. (1928) "Great Britain in Egypt," London, England. Cassell and Co.

Rawdan, Abu Al-Fotouk. (1951) "Old and New Faces in Egyptian Education," Columbia, Washington. Columbia University Press, 1951.

Stevans, G.W. with Rawadan. (1898) "Kitchener to Khartoum," New York, New York. Kodd, Mead, and Co.

Tibawi, A. L. (1972) "Islamic Education, Its Traditions and Modernization into the Arab National Systems," Luzac and Co. Ltd.

Tignor, Robert L. (1966) Modernization and British Colonial Rule in Egypt," Princeton University Press.

White, Arthur Silva. (1899) "The Expansion of Egypt," London, England. Huthen and Co.

Wilson, Florence. (1936) "Near East Educational Survey," London, England. European Center of Carnegie endowment for International Peace, Hogarth Press.

CHAPTER III

NATIONALIZATION OF EDUCATION

1920-1952

Education was a sensitive topic for Egyptian nationalists. Their heritage was an amalgamation of 500 years of Islamic and Coptic kuttabs, 300 years of missionary and language schools, 40 years of continuing British influence, and a variety of state institutions neither uniform nor adequate for the country's needs. So, rather than providing the Egyptians with a single direction for future education, history had provided her with a morass of conflicting educational directions. And, since education in Egypt was neither unified nor comprehensive, the task of nationalizing education had to be derived from this complex heritage.

Egypt's needs were enormous. First, she had to take a largely illiterate rural population and provide them with the rudimentary skills of reading, writing and arithmetic needed as bases for both cultural and technical education. Secondly, she needed to train secular leaders and technicians who could rebuild a country which had been invaded and occupied for 2,000 years and who could move Egypt competitively into the industrial, agricultural and commercial market-place.

The first national effort was toward eradicating illiteracy. In an agrarian society, rural family income was reduced when sons who could work in the fields went to school and paid for books, tuition, and transportation. Furthermore, the curriculum of the elementary schools was perceived as irrelevant when most men worked in the fields and virtually all the women worked in the homes. Schools had been directed by foreigners and had trained for urban occupations which met the needs of the controlling powers. Education had to be made practical, accessible and free in order to encourage attendance.

The new Egyptian constitution of 1923 first mandated that primary education be free and compulsory for all children from 6 to 12. The Ministry of Education then established in the governorates 27 model compulsory schools which terminated at 4th grade level. By 1925, however, the model compulsory schools were abandoned, after the ministry decided to provide education for all by utilizing existing schools. Students in government schools which prepared them for Civil Service positions were then placed on two shifts, morning and afternoon. These schools were also called compulsory schools and in the academic year 1925-1926, 762 such schools remained, although they lacked qualified teachers, adequate facilities, and a unified syllabus. (Harby, 1960, p.21). By 1936, 600 additional compulsory schools had been started. It was determined, however, that compulsory education could not be accomplished in the four years of half-day attendance required. In 1937, all compulsory schools extended the school hours to a full day. The Ministry of Education then realized that any improvement or expansion would be at its own cost and the compulsory education scheme was abandoned. No plan existed which considered the country's conditions and its educational history, materials and population. (Harby, 1960, p.23).

Lack of financial resources further limited Egypt's ability to provide free accessible education. In addition to four-year compulsory schools, the government attempted to expand the number of existing practical schools which had been created for the poor. Called elementary schools, they had consisted of six years and had been considered a complete education. The fifth and sixth grades were to prepare the child for practical life, not through learning a trade, but rather through increasing his interest in practical subjects such as manual skills and farm work. These schools taught no foreign languages and were conducted for a half-day. Administered by both the Ministry of Education and the provincial councils, elementary schools were limited in facilities, curriculum and instruction. Further, they received from the government only 2 pounds per student, as compared to 20 pounds per student in the primary schools. (Boktor, 1936, p.285).

The object of elementary schools was to provide tuition-free education to the masses with great stress on religion, reading, writing and arithmetic.

However, expansion of elementary schools was restricted when the ministry found that the condition of the existing schools was not satisfactory and that the provincial councils did not have the financial resources to permit improvement. Though greater accessibility to schooling had been attempted, the education itself needed improvement. There seemed to be little point in crowding students into poor facilities for years when the end result of reducing illiteracy was not greatly affected. A large number of drop-outs was testimony to the difficulty educating the poor in elementary or compulsory schools.

A second educational need was to provide Egypt with secular leaders to meet her development needs. The primary school, another state system, had previously provided training for secular education. Primary schools had offered a four-year course in which males and females were educated separately, and a tuition fee was charged. Although the fee was abolished in 1943, the history of both governmental and tuition subsidies had provided a basis for this elitist education. Instruction in the primary schools was notably superior to instruction in elementary schools. Even then, the curriculum of primary school, as described by Boktor (1931), was unrelated to the development needs of the country.

> There is a large gap between school and life. The Egyptian school is primarily a place where certain syllabi are covered. Other economic, social, moral or spiritual values are quite secondary or non-existent at all. (p.285).

As they had adequate financial resources, Egyptians living in urban areas were the most likely to begin education in the primary schools.

> The ministry draws to its schools children of the well-to-do who can easily pay the school's, fees and who might have, in other countries, gone to private institutions. The people know that the ministry spends twice as much per child as it receives in payment, consequently those who have influence are sure to send their children to government schools. In other words, the public schools of

Egypt open their doors to the
priviliged citizens for a nominal fee
and leave the poorer children to
attend private schools. (p.199).

Private schools, which were also four years in
length, charged tuition but could not charge more
than government schools; otherwise, they would have
no students. Also, private schools were denied
support unless they followed the governmental
curriculum. According to Boktor, (1936).

They are constantly impoverished by
the ministry, which both provides
subsidies and charges tuition.
Neither a sense of charity or of
public responsibility on the part of
individuals has been developed so as
to endow these institutions with
necessary funds. In Egypt it is only
recently that private institutions
have been recognized as having any
value to the country. Many are still
unfit and far behind the standards of
government schools. (p.200).

As a result of government regulations, the
private schools declined in quality and were limited
in their ability to educate Egyptians for positions
of secular leadership.
Because the primary school graduate had had a
language included in his curriculum, he was able to
pass English and French language sections on the
entrance exam to secondary school, whereas those who
had gone to compulsory elementary schools and
kuttabs had to pay for outside tutoring in order to
pass the language examinations. Clearly, the
country's secular leaders were more likely to be
educated in primary schools. However, even then the
curriculum was not related to the country's
technological or developmental needs. Educational
inconsistency was even more apparent in secondary
schools.
From 1923 through 1952, secondary education was
expanded in order to increase Egypt's capability to
train secular leaders. Commonly regarded as the road
to the university and subsequently to government
posts, high positions, and prestige, the secondary
schools were subjected to great pressure. The
subjects of study were constantly changed with
regard to their number, the content and length of

study. The language of instruction was at all times Arabic, except for teaching the foreign languages, mainly French and English. Some secondary schools were turned into language schools where French, German, Greek, Italian, or English was the instructional language but "national subjects," such as mathematics, science, biology, history, geography, and civics, were and continue to be taught in Arabic. Examination requirements also followed political mandates. During certain administrations, the student had only one chance to pass, while at other times he was allowed several opportunities. Entry to these examinations was also determined by government need. For example, the period of study in secondary education began at three years, became four and then five, was reduced to three, four and, finally, five years in length. The number of required leaders was still dependent upon the number of available government positions. (Harby, 1960, p.48).

Instead of reconsidering the basic policy of secondary education, the ministry opened a large number of new secondary schools which followed a syllabus and system which were themselves in dire need of reform. (El-Hilali, 1935, p.40). Highly qualified, capable teachers were still working in Egypt since the loans to other Arab countries, which drained schools of many of the best teachers, had not reached as large proportions as they did under Nasser. The quality of instruction was very high indeed in some of the best secondary schools of that period, e.g., Saidia, Tewfikiah, Khediviah, Asyut, Abbassia (Alexandria), Ras-el-Tin (Alexandria), and Nokrashy (Cairo). These schools and many others had a distinguished group of eminent teachers and headmasters. Most Egyptian secondary school graduates aspired to enter a university, but in 1923 there was only one national university (The Egyptian University). Al-Azhar had not been reorganized as a university, in spite of its being a renowned seat of traditional Islamic instruction. Higher institutes, such as the French Law School, and the Muslim Judges School, existed, but their enrollment was small. If the graduates of these schools did not find suitable jobs (because very few were available then) this was not the fault of the schools. (Doss, personal interview 1982). It was, rather, the fault of government policy, reflecting the residue of British educational influence.

Furthermore, there was little agreement on how the secular elite should be educated on the secondary level. The desire for a nationalized curriculum was accompanied by confusion in the Egyptian culture. Uncertainty existed about which subjects should be emphasized in the schools. Historically, most Egyptians had been educated in kuttabs whose curriculum had emphasized religion first and then other subjects. But which other subjects? Formerly, the masses were directed by Ulmas and Mameluks, both members of religiously educated ruling classes. Now the society had secular leaders in the form of lawyers, doctors, teachers, journalists, government officials and engineers, each with different interests, tastes, dress, modes of entertainment and, consequently, different ways of thinking. The conflict between religious and secular goals became apparent in secondary schools, where the curriculum consisted of more and more secular subjects added to the already extensive religious instruction and vice versa. There had been two distinct currents of instruction running side by side: the secular, in government and language schools, and the religious, in the religious institutes affiliated to Al-Azhar. These latter were not solely religious, teaching some science, math and social subjects besides Islamic religion and the Arabic language.

The conflict between religious and secular trends in the secondary school curriculum reflected the divided attitudes and loyalities of the country as a whole--modern technology verses Islamic tradition. This dichotomy of the country's loyalities hampered the efforts toward social change and modification of life in the country. The selection of one subject indicated preference for that particular secular field. One curriculum decision could not be made without appearing to deny another part of the transitional Egyptian culture.

In order to nationalize the young Egyptian, both the past and the present had to be accounted for. This resulted in the ossification of the curriculum and methods of instruction. Memorization and formal exams were the most expedient means of covering such a vast amount of material in the short class periods allotted to each subject.

As a result, secondary education was reformed only on matters that did not confront either the secular or religious aspects of the culture. The changes dealt with age of admission to secondary school and procedures for standardizing other post primary studies. (Law 142, 1952). None of the reforms addressed the main concerns identified by the minister of education's criticism of 1935. (El-Halali, 1935, p.45-50). This report cited weakness in school curricula based upon a shifting between general and specialized curricula, continual fluctuation in the examination system, inadequate methods used in language instruction, crowded classrooms, ineffective inspection systems, excessive centralization of administration, ineffective and inadequate teacher training, lack of balance between moral and social education, and reliance upon memorization of facts as a means of acquiring knowledge.

Foreign language schools exemplified the natonalization effort and the fluctuations in educational policy. In 1913, Law 12 prevented foreign language school students from entering institutions of higher education. All students who wanted to study at an Egyptian university had to have a government secondary certificate obtained by passing the "Thanawiya Amma," the graduation exam. However, in 1923, Law 40 allowed missionary, and/or foreign language school students to sit for government exams on the primary and secondary level. At the same time, university and higher institutions continued to admit students who had taken the British General Certificate Exam, provided they took an Arabic exam during their undergraduate years before graduation from university. (Iskandar, 1972, p.15) The numbers of students in these schools were great, as shown in Table 1.

TABLE I

NUMBER OF STUDENTS IN FOREIGN SCHOOLS
1927-28

Number of Schools		TOTAL	MALE	FEMALE
American	78	6,914	2,792	4,122
Italian	91	9,809	4,734	5.075
British	74	4,322	1,953	2,369
French	279	32,812	16,717	16,095
Greek	88	11,396	6,093	5,303
Others	27	3,570	2,871	699
	637	68,823	35,160	33,663

(Boktor, 1963).

The foreign language schools were separate from religious kuttabs and private schools and administered by either embassies or religious missionary groups. Their curriculum and language of instruction directed graduates toward attending higher institutions in the country of their origin. This objective in foreign language education had a serious influence on Egyptian society and national unity. Sizeable groups of relatively well educated Egyptians had a sense of belonging more to the foreign country than to their own. (El-Softi, 1980, p.9).

In 1934, foreign language schools were nationalized. Law 40 mandated that all students in foreign schools, regardless of nationality, were required to learn Arabic, even if they were not preparing to take the government exams. Foreign schools were subject to government supervision; the Ministry of Education was to decide the syllabuses and examinations for all grade levels. And, finally, schools preparing students for government examinations were to follow the ministry's curriculum in civics, history, geography, and Arabic. Foreign language schools could, however, include other curricula if they wished. Also, the law did not specify the language which was to be the medium of instruction. (Salama, 1963, p.15). Finally, in 1955, Law 583 put all language schools under complete supervision of the government, with the country divided into educational zones which were given authority to supervise the Ministry of Education promotion examinations in all subjects. (Rizk, 1981, p.47).

As seen in the legislation directed toward the foreign schools, language instruction and curricula reflected the uncertainty of the Egyptian policies. Foreign language schools added government requirements to their curricula, but continued to offer courses that had existed previously. The curriculum could be either general, technical, or both. Changes in the entrance requirements for the national government exam and criteria for passing also affected these schools. After 1934, foreign schools had to meet Egyptian administration requirements, but they were still affiliated with parent organizations. Thus, while Arabic was taught in all language schools, French, English, German, Greek or Italian remained the language of instruction.

Once graduated from the language or goverment secondary schools, students could attend the university. The National University was taken over by the government on March 11, 1925, and placed under separate administration because the Ministry of Education had not adequately financed the university and prevented it from expanding or meeting the requirements of scientific research. Thus, the university had been compelled to limit its activities to literary studies. The university had remained in existence due to the Ministry of Wakfs and donations from the population, which enabled it to employ a number of foreign professors acting as visiting lecturers rather than permanent faculty.

The decree establishing the Egyptian State University in 1925 provided for faculties of arts, science, medicine (including pharmacy) and law. The new university later incorporated the existing schools of medicine and of law and made the National University, into the Faculty of Arts. The law further obligated the university to encourage scientific research and to work for the promotion of arts and science in the country. Egypt now had two complete national educational systems.

The poor Egyptians entered the elementary school or kuttab and could continue their education at Al-Azhar, or in vocational training schools. The richer student attended the primary schools or foreign language school and completed their education in the National University or abroad.

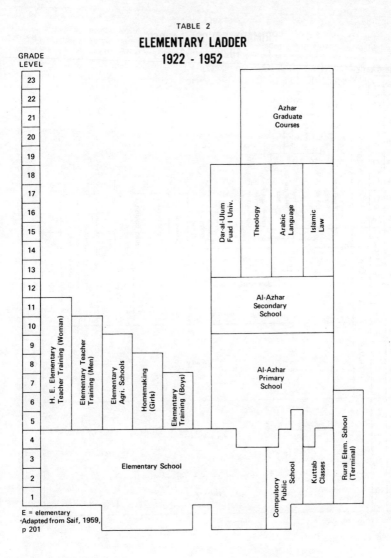

TABLE 2

ELEMENTARY LADDER
1922 - 1952

GRADE LEVEL

| 23 |
| 22 |
| 21 |
| 20 |
| 19 |
| 18 |
| 17 |
| 16 |
| 15 |
| 14 |
| 13 |
| 12 |
| 11 |
| 10 |
| 9 |
| 8 |
| 7 |
| 6 |
| 5 |
| 4 |
| 3 |
| 2 |
| 1 |

Azhar Graduate Courses

Dar-al-Ulum Fuad I Univ.

Theology

Arabic Language

Islamic Law

Al-Azhar Secondary School

Al-Azhar Primary School

H. E. Elementary Teacher Training (Woman)

Elementary Teacher Training (Men)

Elementary Agri. Schools

Homemaking (Girls)

Elementary Training (Boys)

Elementary School

Compulsory Public School

Kuttab Classes

Rural Elem. School (Terminal)

E = elementary
Adapted from Saif, 1959, p 201

TABLE 3

PRIMARY SCHOOL LADDER
1922 - 1952

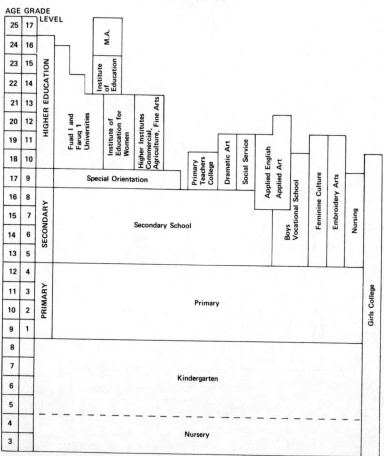

Adapted from Saif, 1959, p. 202

Each primary, elementary, and secondary educational system was administered by random, adjunct or separate units which limited educational reform. Other complete systems were found in foreign language, religious and private schools, all separately administered. Opportunities for graduates to move up the educational ladder were much greater for primary students than for those who attended vocational, religious, compulsory or elementary schools. (Boktor, 1963, p.78). And each stage of the educational sequence had a pressing need for reform which could only be accomplished through a unified administrative structure.

The only form of co-operation that existed between the groups of primary and elementary institutions in Egypt was the annual financial aid granted by the Ministry of Education to those schools that conformed to certain standards and opened their doors to government inspectors. Other schools were not in any way related to government schools and there existed neither co-operation nor mutual exchange of ideas. (Boktor, 1963, p.79).

To unify the six types of elementary and primary schools, the elite primary graduates were required to pass an Arabic language exam, and in 1943 tuition fees were abolished. These changes were cosmetic, however, rather than substantive. In practice, both elementary and primary schools remained as divergent in facilities, utilities, and teachers as they had been before nationalization attempts were made. Egyptian parents still recognized the superior quality of primary schools. From 1940 to 1952, enrollment doubled for primary schools with no growth at all for elementary schools. (Harby, 1960, p.75).

Teacher training reflected negative aspects of government centralization. When the Ministry of Education wanted to extend the scope of education, it had to train teachers. By 1927, 25 training schools existed for men, and 18 for women. According to Boktor (1931), "For a girl of the poorest class it is more honorable to beg than to work. In upper Egypt, to be a school teacher is the last resort for any girl who is not the daughter of a pauper or a coachman." (Boktor 1931, p.75). In order to find enough teachers for the compulsory educational project, the ministry created evening classes for men which provided training on a provisional basis. A one-year course of study was offered in these classes for applicants who had passed the elementary courses in religious institutions or held primary proficiency certificates. All applicants had to pass a test in the Koran, Arabic, calligraphy, arithmetic, and geography which paralleled the curriculum of the second year syllabus in the male teacher training schools. These classes were cancelled in 1927 after the teacher training institutes started graduating an adequate number of teachers. (Harby, 1960, p.54).

In 1929, the ministry tried to raise the standard of male teacher training institutes by setting up special schools to prepare entrants. This meant that a two-year course of study in teacher training followed the completion of six years of elementary education. However, the number of special schools decreased as a result of the ministry's prolonged delay in carrying out the plan. This delay resulted in the over-production of less qualified graduates from elementary male and female teacher training schools. Thus, the number of special teacher training schools decreased from 25 to eight for men and from 18 to seven for women by 1938. (Harby, 1960, p.55). During this time, no specific training was required for teaching in most schools, and graduates of higher institutes and universities taught in primary and secondary schools. Teacher training expanded and contracted based upon immediate needs as perceived by the Ministry of Education.

Finally, financial allocations for teacher training, salaries, curriculum development, and educational expansion were not very generous. The salaries of the high officials in all the 10 ministries, including the Ministry of Education, were extravagant for the time. (Boktor, 1963, p.53). However, considering that the country needed to quicken its pace of progress in literacy and development of leaders, the educational budget was too small relative to the general budget.

TABLE 4

PROPORTION OF THE EDUCATIONAL BUDGET TO THE TOTAL BUDGET IN

VARIOUS COUNTRIES

Country		Proportion of Educational Budget to Total Budget
Spain	(1927)	5.2 %
France	(1927)	5.49%
Czechoslovakia	(1926)	6.1 %
Belgium	(1926)	6.5 %
Italy	. (1926)	6.66%
Great Britain	(1926)	7.00%
China	(1931)	10.00%
Rumania	(1926)	11.4 %
Bulgaria	(1926)	11.7 %
Norway	(1926)	13.7 %
Denmark	(1926)	14.2 %
Holland	(1926)	19.3 %
Geneva	(1928)	30.00%
Egypt	(1930)	7.3 %

Dr. Ed. Claparede's Report, p.100 (Arabic) and League of Nations'
Report on China, p.50.

Egypt did not compare favourably with other countries when the financial resources of the other countries were taken into account. Even her small expenditures were not evenly proportioned. Annual cost per pupil, in round numbers, was two Egyptian pounds in the elementary, 20 in the primary, and 40 in the secondary school. This enormous difference between the money expended per pupil from elementary to secondary (1 to 20) or primary to secondary (1 to 2) was something unheard of, considering that in Europe the ratio of the cost per pupil in a primary school to that per student in a university was 1 to 8 or 1 to 10. (Khanky, 1958, p.141-3). The cost per pupil in elementary as compared to primary and secondary school stood in close relation to the difference in the scale of teachers' salaries. While the ratio between an elementary and primary school teacher salary ranged between 1 to 3 and 1 to 6, and that between the primary and the secondary ranged from 1 to 2 and 1 to 3. (Khanky, 1958, p.141-3).

In summary, nationalization of Egyptian education focused on the expansion of literacy, the development of secular leaders and the unification of the education system. In order to make education available to all, elementary schooling was mandated in 1922. The number of schools was increased and the length of the school day expanded. Tuition was abolished. However, each of these efforts was limited by inadequate allocation of financial resources, which indicated a lack of financial commitment on the part of the government toward education.

The development of secular leaders was conducted through the primary, secondary and university educational system, while religious leaders were educated in kuttabs and Al-Azhar University. The question remained as to which competencies and skills Egyptians needed. The result was that curriculum fluctuated with political policy. Length of study and criteria for entering or existing schools remained dependent upon government employment needs for secular occupations. Foreign language schools mirrored the confusion of the period as they continued to educate students to identify with two cultures and government schools attempted to instruct students in all areas. Hence, no clear sense of a national curriculum emerged during this period.

TABLE 5

Secondary School Exams
1922-1954

Years in School

Years in School	1922 (3 years)	1926–1936 (4 years)	1936–1954 (4 years)	1954 (5 years)
1	Secondary School Exam I		Secondary School Exam I	
2	Secondary School Exam I	Secondary School Exam I	Secondary School Exam I	
3	Secondary School Exam II	Secondary School Exam I	Secondary School Exam I	Secondary School Exam I
4		Secondary School Exam II	Secondary School Exam II	Secondary School Exam I
5				Secondary School Exam II

Personal Interview, Dr. Yousif Kotb

All educational systems--foreign, private, religious and public--needed to be unified with a single national purpose. While national control of examinations served to standardize instruction, the content of the courses and secular or religious emphasis continued to be in conflict. Teacher training was expanded or contracted based upon the changing emphasis of the Ministry of Education and reflecting government needs rather than educational pedagogy. Further, the co-operation of all schools within fluctuating policies determined financial allocations. The financial needs of the schools and the employment of the government contributed to an educational process in a constant state of flux. By 1952, the unification of the educational systems was complete, although an analysis of the national budget revealed insufficient financial allocations to meet most educational needs.

Perhaps the educational needs were too great during this period to be met adequately. By 1930, enrollment of the childeren in the government schools of Egypt had increased to 18 percent, including both elementary and primary institutions. Compared with China's 21 percent, Turkey's 25 percent, and Russia's 82 percent, this number appeared small. The number of girls in all government institutions was 40 percent that of boys. If elementary education was omitted from consideration, the proportion of females dropped to 13 percent. (Boktor, 1936, p.196). However, when compared with the 3 1/2 percent of primary age students enrolled in the late 1800's, the expansion was significant.

From 1882 to 1922, The British had claimed that too many other needs demanded attention before educational reform. It was evident that a great deal of attention had been directed toward education in the form of legislative and ministerial decrees. The educational changes occurring between 1922 and 1952 had taken place despite political and economic turmoil as full of conflict as the 1982-1922 period. British troops had never left Egypt and their presence and increased numbers infuriated the Egyptians. During World War II, British had trained Egyptians to be military officers. These young Egyptian officers, including Gamal Abdul Nasser and Anwar Sadat, formed clandestine groups of "Free Officers" who plotted and fomented internal disruption.

The British and conscripted Egyptians, on the other hand, spent much of World War II fighting the

North African Allied campaign in Egypt. Italian and German troops invaded Egypt attempting to capture the Suez Canal. The Italians fought in Egypt in 1940 and 1941 before they were driven out by the British, only to have the Germans invade in 1941. Anwar Sadat attempted to arrange a military _coup_ with the Germans but the plot failed. British and German fighting continued through 1942 increasing the turmoil in the country. In an effort to align with both the Arab countries and Allied forces, Egypt became a charter member of both the United Nations, and the Arab League. When the U.N. voted in 1947 to divide Palestine into Jewish and Arab nations, the Arab League voted to invade Israel. Egypt was caught in the middle between U.N. and Arab League decisions and chose to invade Israel. The United Nations ended most of the fighting by 1949 and arranged for Egypt and Israel to sign an armistice. But a state of war continued between Egypt and Israel because no peace treaty was signed. In 1950, Egypt blocked Israeli ships from using the Suez Canal, escalating the terrorism and combat between the two countries. By 1952, Egypt and had been involved in two world wars, invaded by Germans, Italians, French and occupied by the British. Internally, the Turkish khedive or king had had little effect upon the government which remained unstable. And, through it all, the life of most Egyptians had continued much the same as it had been for the past 600 years. Farming, family, religion, and conscription into the army remained at the center of his life. His educational needs and his educational opportunities had been minimal. Considering how long Egypt had been under foreign rule, the growth of education was credible, but insufficient to the developing needs of the country.

Independence was still incomplete. Egyptians continued to live under British military occupation. Popular anger at a dissolute king, corrupt party politicians, and an ineffective parliament led to growing unrest, riots, demonstrations and the rise of a group of revolutionary army officers. The old order had proved itself unfit to govern Egypt, in educational policy and every other way. The final result was the 1952 revolution.

CHAPTER III REFERENCES

Boktor, Amir. (1931). "Education for Life," Cairo, U.A.R. Mukattam Press.

Boktor, Amir. (1936) "School and Society in the Valley of the Nile," Cairo, U.A.R. Elias Modern Press.

Boktor, Amir. (1963) "The Development and Expansion of Education in the United Arab Republic," Cairo, U.A.R. American University in Cairo Press.

Dr. El-Softi, Madiha. (1980) "Foreign Education in the Arab World: Duality of National Education and the problems of Belonging." Unpublished doctorial dissertation, Ain Shams University, Cairo, Egypt.

El-Hilali, Ahmed Naguib. (1935) "Secondary Education: Its Defects and Ways and Means of Reform," Cairo, U.A.R.

Harby, Mohammed. (1960) "Education in United Arab Republic in the Twentieth Century," Cairo. General Organization for Government Printing.

Iskandar, H. (1972). Problems of Bilingual Education in English Schools in Egypt. Paper presented at the meeting of Teaching of English as Second Language (March).

Khanky Bey, Aziz, (1958) "Egyptian Problems." Mukattam Press.

Rizk, Nazli Hanna. (1981) "Factors Affecting the Standard of Achievement in English of Student in English Language Schools in Egypt," Unpublished master's thesis. American University in Cairo.

Saif, Phillip. (1958) "Egyptian Education: Descriptive Study." Unpublished doctoral thesis, University of Michigan.

Salama, G. (1963) "Tarikh el taalim al agnabi fi misr, (The History of Education in Egypt)." Cairo, U.A.R.. University Dissertation Publishers.

CHAPTER IV

SOCIALIZATION OF EDUCATION

1952-1970

In 1952, the Egyptian army seized control of
the country. Their first action was to oust King
Farouk and dissolve parliament. The popular
commander of and chief of the army, Mohammed Naguib,
became president and head of Revolutionary Command
Council. As the first Egyptian ruler in centuries,
he demonstrated a concern for the masses. From 1952
to 1956 there was justification for the belief that
the country's domestic problems of poverty,
illiteracy and disease would become the government's
primary concern.

The Free Officers who composed the
Revolutionary Council and power of the government
acted immediately to pass many reform laws, the most
notable of which was the agrarian law of September
1952, giving confiscated land to the peasant
families in lots of 2 to 5 feddans with each feddan
equal to 1.038 acres. The right of all to own land
reduced taxable revenue and diminished the economic
and political power of the big landowners. Having
money became dangerous, and those who were wealthy
no longer displayed it in educational contributions,
life styles, or habits. Children of the rich and
poor alike flooded into the schools as education was
the right of all Egyptians. Private schools,
formerly a means of education for some of the
wealthy, decreased in enrollments and in revenues.

Prior to the 1952 revolution, educational
issues resulted from Egypt's cumbersome, disunited
educational system and reflected the political,
economic, and social conditions of the country. With
the revolution, socialism became the framework for
governing and was reflected in the educational
philosophy. The implementation of this philosophy
greatly altered the schools. Administration was

centralized, curriculum was standardized, enrollment escalated and technical education was emphasized. All were designed to promote the development of Egyptian patriotism through education of the masses.

Education of the masses expanded in 1953 when a new primary school system was legislated abolishing the former elementary school system. Like the elementary school legislated in 1922, the new primary school was supposed to eradicate illiteracy and was free and compulsory for boys and girls from 6 to 12. In 1952, one million pupils were enrolled in primary schools. A decade later found over three million students in the same schools. Unfortunately, the buidings and facilities had not increased or been improved at the same rate. (Boktor, 1963, p.204). In theory, everyone had a right to education, but the limited space available placed practical contraints on that right. In education as in other areas of state policy, the major changes came, not with the 1952 coup, but in the following years. This was the real Egyptian revolution, guided, not by Naguib, but by Gamal Abdel Nasser.

Nasser, though born in Alexandria, came from a family that retained its ties to Upper Egypt. Upper Egyptians, called Saidis, used to be scorned by their more sophisticated Cairo compatriots and even by the peasants from the Delta, although they also had a reputation for strength, courage, and close ties with the desert Arab tribesmen. Throughout his Presidency Nasser remained simple in his life style thus maintaining an affinity with his people. Educated in government schools, Nasser had been an ardent nationalist since his youth. As a result of the opening of the military academy in 1936 to young men who could pass a competitive examination, Nasser was able to become an officer in the Egyptian army. He quickly saw that Egypt's independence was a sham, since the British remained in effective control. But neither civilian politicians, Muslim Brothers, nor Communists had the cohesion needed to win Egypt's freedom and reform its society. Only a secret society of army officers whom Nasser called Free Officers could overthrow the corrupt regime and attain these patriotic goals. For ten years, Nasser gathered around him a group of young officers, including Anwar Sadat, until the time was ripe to strike. General Naguib served as a popular figure-head, but once the Revolutionary Command Council began to issue reform decrees, it proved to be Nasser who really controlled the Revolutionary Council. Finally, in February 1954, he challenged

Naguib and his backers openly, and managed, owing mainly to the loyalty of his fellow officers, to replace him as president.

By October of 1954, the Egyptian public realized that Colonel Gamal Abdul Nasser had become the actual leader of the country. The same month, the British acceded to Egyptian demands and agreed to remove their troops by June 18, 1956. Foreign companies and schools became unpopular as the Egyptian educational system reflected the political philosophy of Nasser known as Arab socialism. Initially, the military government was viewed as temporary until the people could assume control. But by 1956, this expectation faded, as the military regime showed no signs of relinquishing its power, and Nasser was elected president supported by the Revolutionary Council. Wealthy Egyptians and foreigners who had previously managed the country watched as their companies and property were confiscated through the nationalization of industry and land. As companies were nationalized, previous business leaders retreated into inconsequential jobs, departed or refused to work altogether, many not wishing to be employees in their own companies. Military leaders moved into this leadership vacuum. Military officers served as ministers in all strategic departments and as second level administrators in technical ministeries headed by civilians, controlling the decision making in most state administrations. Thus, government, business, defense and, most significantly, education came under military leadership.

Military influence extended into the curriculum. Military training was added to the curriculum and the military became the career for many young Egyptians. The Arabic language was more important than any other subject on national exams. Students could fail in two subjects and still be promoted provided they passed their Arabic exam with a minimum of 50 percent. (Risk, 1981, p.30). Prior to that time, it was possible for Egyptians to attend foreign schools and universities within the country, enabling them to become proficient in the history, customs and language of another country without attaining proficiency in Arabic. Education in Arabic and military subjects became tools to unify the country.

> I sometimes consider the state of the
> average Egyptian family--one of thou-
> sands of families which live in the

the capital of the country. The
father, for example, is a turbanned
fellah--a thoroughbred country
fellow. The mother is a lady of
Turkish descent. The sons and
daughters attend schools respectively
folowing English and French
educational systems. With this is an
atmosphere where the 13th century
spirit and 20th century manifestations manifestations intermingle and
interact. We live in a society not
yet crystalized. It is still in a
state of ferment and agitation. It is
not yet stabilized in its gradual
development compared with people who
passed before on the same road.
(Nasser, 1954, p.41).

The nationalization of the Suez Canal in 1956
reinforced the power of Nasser and of the military.
Nasser had challenged the Western countries for
leadership in the Arab world. His purchase of arms
from communist Czechoslovakia in 1955, his
nationalism of the Suez Canal Company and defiance
of the tripartite invasion of Egypt by Britain,
France and Israel in 1956, and his union with Syria
to form the United Arab Republic in 1958, combined
to make him a hero, not only to Egyptians, but to
Arabs everywhere. While the nationalization of the
Suez Canal was not an overwhelming military success,
the military was able to take over the canal and
keep it in operation. The concept of the Egyptian
army as a force in Egypt and other Arab countries
seemed viable. The ideal of Egyptian leadership and
military power extended beyond Egyptian borders.
Developing Egyptian influence now involved Nasser in
regional quarrels, not only in the Arab-Israeli
conflicts, but in many inter-Arab quarrels. Prestige
factors sometimes proved more important than the
Egyptian people who had pressing domestic needs.
Rather than education, the Yemini war and other
concerns related to patriotism dictated policy.
Egypt was in a constant state of war, aiding other
Arab countries in removing British or French rule.
Egypt as the most populous country in the
Middle East, became the leading military and
educational force in the area. In March of 1958,
Yemen joined Egypt and Syria and the three countries
became the United Arab States. All Arabs and Moslems
could be educated in Egypt at Egyptian expense. In

1959-60, there were 14,349 foreign students representing 57 countries studying at different schools and colleges in Egypt. Of these, 2,259 students were studying at the expense of the Egyptian government; their board and other expenses cost the Ministry of Education L.E.241,000, an expense Egypt could not afford. Moreover, Egyptian teachers were loaned to 14 countries in Africa and Asia. In 1961-62, for example, 300 urgently needed teachers were loaned to foreign elementary and secondary schools and universities. Both the exporting of teachers and the education of Arabs from other countries involved the state in considerable expense with no visible material return. (Boktor, 1963, p.198). And the numbers kept growing; 349 foreign students in 1959-60 expanded to 20,878 by 1961. The country was already confronting serious economic problems stemming from lack of capital, inadequate planning and an ineffective bureaucratic structure. These problems were now reflected in the educational system.

Predictably, the emphasis on obtaining an education at a foreign school in Egypt declined. Before the British, French and Israelis invaded the Suez Canal, 97,000 students were enrolled in foreign language schools. After the invasion, the number declined by 17,000. British and French teachers left and foreign schools were closed from October 29, 1956, to January 10, 1957. All foreign schools were sequestered except for American schools and those which were under Vatican administration. The American University in Cairo remained open but was placed under close Egyptian governmental supervision. Egyptian teachers already employed had to take extra loads to meet the crisis. Others were hired who were not qualified to teach. Consequently, instruction in foreign language and government schools began to decline and continued to do so. (Iskander, 1972, p.11). Furthermore, the number of students in all private schools declined to a low of 46,800 by 1960. Because government schools were open to all and free of charge, they absorbed students from private and foreign schools into increasingly overcrowded conditions.

Although the nationalization of foreign schools tended to assure the uniformity of Egypt's educational system, its quality suffered because of the great expense of the Nasser government's foreign and military policies. The struggle to remove British and French colonialist influence from southern Arabia and northern Africa proved costly,

45

especially when Egypt got involved in a five-year civil war in Yemen. The cost of Soviet weapons and of maintaining Egyptian troops abroad drained the Egyptian government of resources, even as capital was scarce, planning was indaquate, and the bureaucracy was inefficient. The result was that Egypt's educational system was neglected.

One of the country's most urgent needs at this time was to train Egyptians to replace the foreign technicians expelled after nationalization of the Suez Canal in 1956. Expansion of the primary schools continued, along with the immediate initiation of preparatory and secondary technical schools. Both the preparatory and secondary schools were three years in length and led to higher technical education. Five years after the Suez Canal take-over and the resulting political emphasis on the status of technical education, the number of students increased from 8,000 to 42,000 in preparatory school, from 22,000 to 75,000 in secondary schools, and from 1,400 to 15,000 in higher technical institutions. (Boktor, 1963, p.205). The graduates of these institutions formed an elite technocratic civilian element which increased in prominence after the socialist legislation in 1961 and 1962 which expanded the public sector and created a great need for qualified Egyptians to fill a wide variety of technical positions.

As preparation for these positions, science was emphasized in the secondary schools and universities. In the National Charter of 1962, Nasser described science as the weapon with which revolutionary triumph could be achieved. During the first year of secondary school, all students followed the same program; in the second year they branched out into either literary or scientific specialization. The majority were encouraged to join the scientific course in order to specialize in physics, mathematics, chemistry and biology. Secondary school was either academic or technical and professional. But of the ministry's total 1960-61 budget of L.E.58 million, less than three million, or 6.7 percent, went to secondary education--a reflection of a steady decrease of government expenditure on general secondary schools compared to the 1955 budget of 11.7 percent. (Boktor, 1963, p.206). The emphasis on technical education, however, necessitated the increase of support from 4.8 percent of the total educational budget to 9.5 percent. (Boktor, 1963, p.207). Technical education expanded, but it did so at the expense of general secondary education.

Unfortunately, the technical education provided did not adequately prepare students. Lack of qualified teachers was aggravated by the policy of exporting teachers and deporting foreign teachers. Secondly, technical education of any quality could not be initiated without laboratories, equipment and space. Furthermore, the issue of training technical experts to operate in a society that was agrarian in nature was not adequately addressed. While technical education was emphasized, the cost of implementing the necessary changes remained an impediment to the quality of the education. Capital needed for education was directed toward military efforts and defense.

Egypt's defeat in the June 1967 war set back progress in state educational development, as government funds had to be diverted to rebuilding the army and air force, much of which had been destroyed by the Israeli's or dissipated in the long Yemen Civil War. It is estimated that the government's direct military outlay reached five billion pounds between 1967 and 1974. (Hyde, 1978, p.213). Clearly military needs were given priority over domestic needs of education.

TABLE 6

UNIFIED EDUCATIONAL LADDER 1979

AL-AZHAR side (left):

HIGHER EDUCATION INSTITUTES AND COLLEGES
- Fine Arts
- Physical Education
- Dar al-Ulum
- Law
- Education
- Social Service
- Medicine
- Agriculture

SECONDARY — Technical
- Industrial
- Commercial
- Agricultural
- Teacher Training Institutes

SECONDARY — General
- Science
- Literary

PREPARATORY
- Industrial
- Commercial
- Agricultural
- General

PRIMARY

Left margin boxes: AL-AZHAR UNIVERSITY · AL-AZHAR SECONDARY · AL-AZHAR PREPARATORY · AL-AZHAR PRIMARY

Other side (right):

HIGHER EDUCATION INSTITUTES AND COLLEGES
- Commerce
- Engineering
- Veterinary
- Dentistry
- Applied Arts
- Higher Institutes for Teacher Training
- Higher Industrial Institutes

SECONDARY — Technical
- Teacher Training Institute
- Commercial
- Agricultural
- Industrial

SECONDARY — General
- Science
- Literary

PREPARATORY
- Post Primary Terminal
- Oriental Music
- Technical-Girls

PRIMARY

Central data table:

TOTAL IN AGE GROUP	TOTAL ENROLMENT MALE	GRADE	TOTAL ENROLMENT FEMALE	TOTAL IN AGE GROUP
		18		
		17		
		16		
		15		
		14		
		13		
424,000	199,100	12	116,602	407,000
439,000	180,387	11	106,529	422,000
451,000	218,446	10	130,667	434,000
459,000	375,260	9	208,140	442,000
465,000	293,478	8	173,201	448,000
471,000	310,888	7	186,341	454,000
477,000	328,770	6	199,089	460,000
484,000	387,911	5	241,313	467,000
493,000	469,192	4	297,672	475,000
503,000	431,890	3	286,339	483,000
512,000	507,673	2	344,579	491,000
524,000	464,572	1	328,500	501,000

Adapted from World Bank report 21139
Amir Boktor, American University in Cairo Press, 1963, U.A.R.

Education was compulsory; yet, instead of more than 4 million primary school age children attending school, just over three million did so, of whom less than a million were girls. This was an increase of more than a million from 1952. However, this first step of the educational ladder was severely restricted by a lack of facilities and teachers, for only 20 percent of the primary graduates could be absorbed into preparatory schools. Teacher training programs for scientific and technical courses as well as classes for preparatory and secondary teachers were increased. From 1960 to 1965, L.E.4,320,000 was spent on training teachers for preparatory, general and technical education, a figure which represented 6.5 percent of total educational expenditure for that period. The emphasis in the educational expenditure was overwhelmingly on technical and primary education.

Despite various difficulties, the educational ladder was unified by 1970. At nearly every level, the student was required to pass a standardized state exam as a prerequisite for admission to the next level. Failure meant that occupational choice was restricted. Because of the numbers of applicants, few additional chances were provided for re-examination.

Unification on the primary level was achieved by the Ministry of Education, the curriculum and the textbooks. Instruction was further standardized by the sixth grade examination. Since there was continuity and standardization, costs were reduced. However, a negative aspect was the continuation of tendencies toward memorization of the textbook and a disinterest in any change toward improved teaching methods which did not directly help prepare for the exam. Another problem was the great demand for teachers, which meant that out of necessity, many unqualififed teachers with less than 14 years of education on the preparatory or intermediate level were hired.

Several paths were open to those who entered preparatory school. The highest scoring students were encouraged to attend preparatory schools which led to university and higher institute secondary schools. Other preparatory schools trained in industrial, commercial and technical areas. Still a third group of preparatory schools emphasized post-primary work, music, technical training for girls in home economics, public and private health administration, and physical education. It was estimated that about 45 percent of preparatory students were allowed to continue their education in general, technical or specialized secondary programs.

Those who attended secondary schools had been encouraged to concentrate on science and technology. The government provided a greater number of openings and better pay to those secondary students who majored in science rather than literature. Since fewer students could actually handle the more difficult scientific and technical areas (as opposed to the social sciences), there was an over-abundance of social scientists who had fewer job opportunities to begin with. Consequently, a large cadre was formed of graduates who were dissatisfied with the results of their educational efforts, despite the fact that the socialized system guaranteed them a job.

Furthermore, the expansion of secondary programs aggravated an already serious unemployment problem, as general program graduates were not accepted to higher education and entered the socialized economy. Without further training, they had meager technical know-how which was difficult to utilize. However, as "educated" persons they would not do manual labor. Teaching became a last resort; instructors entered teaching who were trained in other areas and thus lacked motivation for teaching.

The Nasser regime had emphasized the right of education for all. The schools had expanded enrollment on all levels and particularly in scientific and technological education. Like Mohammed Ali, Nasser had needed technicians and scientists to support the military. But he had had a broader vision of the value of technologists and had seen them as leaders in the development of the country. After the 1957 war, he had expelled Western technicians and rejected their financial aid but found that he needed Soviet technologists and military financing to replace them.

Further, his reliance on the military had influenced not only the leadership of the country but also the curriculum of the schools. Military courses were taught along with the regular curriculum. The military was a tool to reinforce the concept of Egyptian patriotism. Common language, culture and religion underscored the fact that the Arab countries were all sufferers from occupation by Britian, France or Italy. Nasser's emphasis on nationalism was, in the first place, a reaction to Western influence and, at the same time, an expression of genuine faith in the potential of the

Egyptian people. "Young people will become the dominant factor in the Arab countries. Education is spreading everywhere and this will change things. There may be a leap--or a dialogue--no one knows." (Stephens, 1972, p.559). To emphasize Egyptian power, Nasser shared Egypt's resources. The loan of teachers to Arab countries was motivated by a sense of confidence in Egyptian education over Egypt's Arab sisters who were then just awakening to the need for spreading modern education. It was also due to a sense of Egypt's responsibility to enlighten them. Thus, the loan of teachers to Arab countries and the influx of Arab students began and continued. The schools were overwhelmed by the increasing number of native and foreign students, accompanied by the diminishing number and quality of teachers. The fact that the schools functioned at all under such conditions was a testimony to the commitment of Egyptian people and, most specifically, Egyptian educators.

In short, Egypt had been in a constant state of war from 1948 to 1970. As the most populous country in the Middle East, she provided armies for surrounding Moslem countries as they fought Israeli, French, British and Italian forces. Furthermore, Egypt had provided shelter and fought for the Palestinians including a major war against the Israelis in 1967. During that war, all her air force and most of her army except those who had been fighting in Yemen, were destroyed. The Egyptian soldiers returned from Yemen and became a cadre of terrorists and soldiers to battle the Israelis. Military efforts had destroyed the economy and stability of the country.

In theory, Arab socialism offered the possibility of badly needed improvements--land, housing, education and employment for all. Egyptian education should be free, available to everyone, unified in language, curriculum, administration and evaluation. These values were shared by many other countries--Western, oriental and Eastern. But the manner of implementing socialism theory at a time when Egypt lacked resources exacted great toll from the people.

Each year 600,000 new workers entered the labor force and were absorbed by artifically expanding positions and government subsidies necessary in order for the people to survive on their salaries. Instead of the family and landowners supporting the poor, the government became the supporter of everyone. And this support was extended to other

Arab neighbors.

So, while Nasser remained an idol to the rest of the Arab world, his use of military force and Arab nationalism to implement a unified philosophy overwhelmed Egyptian education. The elite-masses dichotomy had been destroyed in favor of mass secular education of questionable quality. Reduction of illiteracy in order to enable agrarian Egytians to adapt and use technology had been attempted but facilities and qualified instructors were lacking. One value, that of Arab unity had been implemented through manditory military courses, and service and Arabic language emphasis. The theory seemed humanitarian, but its implementation had proved unmanageable. Another philosophy, the Open Door Policy, with concurrent capitalism, was utilized by Sadat to improve Egypt's educational system.

CHAPTER IV REFERENCES

Boktor, Amir: (1963). "The Development and Expansion of Education in the United Arab Republic," Cairo, U.A.R. American University in Cairo press.

Hyde, Georgie D. M. (1973). "Education in Modern Egypt, Ideals and Realities," London, England. Routledge and Kegan Paul.

Iskander, H. (1972). "Problems of Bilingual Education in English Schools in Egypt." TEFL paper. (March)

Naser, Famal Abdel. (1954). "Philosophy of Revolution," Cairo, U.A.R.

Rizk, Nazli Hanna: (1981). "Factors Affecting the Standard of Achievement in English of Student in English Language Schools in Egypt," unpublished master's thesis, American University in Cairo, Cairo.

Stephens, Robert Henry: (1972). "Nasser: A Political Biography," New York, N.Y., Simon and Schuster.

CHAPTER V

THE OPEN DOOR EDUCATIONAL POLICY

1970 - 1981

        With Nasser's death in 1970, Anwar Sadat
inherited a country in economical and educational
crisis. Education for the masses remained a top
priority, but there were financial difficulties. To
increase Egypt's economical and educational base,
Sadat challenged the newly established social
equality. He adopted the open door policy of
inviting foreign investors to stimulate development.
The foreign investors were mostly Western, as there
was an Arab consensus against Egypt and her pro-
Israeli moves begun with the Camp David agreement.
(Maddy-Weitzman, 1981, p.389) By inviting in foreign
investors, Sadat brought back the foreign ruler-
Egyptian poor dichotomy into the culture.
Materially, most Egyptians lived on a much lower
scale than foreigners. When the government reduced
subsidies on food and fuel in 1977, the people
rioted and the government acquiesced adopting a
mixed economy--part socialistic, part capitalistic.
History repeated itself. The poor Egyptians sought
comfort in religious fundamentalism. Symbolic of the
people's patriotism was the increase in the number
of veiled women on the streets of Cairo and
Alexandria. The pro-populous movements were split
between the illegal communist party and the Muslim
Brotherhood. Once again the religious and cultural
heritage clashed with the lifestyle of wealthy
Egyptian and foreign participants in the open door
program who were for the most part American, German,
French, and Japanese.
        The educational system now reflected the mixed
economy and divided culture. The Egyptians who were
unable or unwilling to be educated in foreign
schools attended the overcrowded government schools.
Their education reflected the poverty of the masses

and although foreign investment was apparent, they received few benefits. Egyptian teachers needed better facilities and equipment. Graduates of these schools, regardless of skill, were guaranteed low-paying government jobs and placed wherever the government needed them. Cairo-trained doctors and dentists went to the Sinai or rural hospitals where their monthly salary of L.E.70 maintained them at a subsistence level. Graduates of foreign language schools with French, English, or German competency got high-paying jobs in the private sector. A beginning secretary in a government position made L.E.70 a month, while an English-speaking secretary in a foreign company could start as high as L.E.350. The foreign, private schools once again became the means of attaining higher economic and social status.

In September 1973, a full-scale war erupted between Arab countries - including Egypt - and Israel. Egypt regained some of her territory in the Sinai before an Egyptian-Israeli ceasefire was signed in November 1973. The war was viewed as a victory by the Egyptian people and Sadat was legitimized as the country's leader, even though his re-introduction of foreigners into the country and his personal lifestyle identified him as a representative of the rich Westerners. Foreign affiliated Egyptians became wealthy as attending a foreign school and speaking a foreign language became the ticket to increased income. But foreign schools had not educated these Egyptians to have a concern for the poor with whom they shared neither common values, language nor social status. So while there were more Mercedes in Cairo than in Dallas, completed telephone calls, sugar and potable water were luxuries for others. "The Egyptian economy has virtually collapsed; Cairo is physically disintegrating; the population's standard of living has declined while a small portion of businessmen and managerial elite prospers. There are, it is said, more millionaires today than ever before." (Pierre, 1978 p.155).

The Egyptian educational system was doing the very best it could to both solicit outside funding for facilities, equipment, training and to increase the enrollment of its youth, particularly in primary educational institutions. The following description never before published outside Egypt, reflects both the concern and the financial needs of primary education. In 1980, the National Council, an advisory board to the president of Egypt, reported the following:

1) The annual total cost per pupil is L.E.28.8 per year (LE1 = approximately $1), of which L.E.20.5 is appropriated for wages with the pupil actually receiving approximately L.E. 9 per year.

2) There is an excess of 10,000 teachers of some specializations, most of whom have not received educational training and a "grave shortage" of classroom teachers.

3) 48.8 percent of the teachers have been trained in teacher-training institutes. The rest are not certified.

4) There is a discrepancy between the required 846 class periods and the 648 actually taught.

5) Of the total 8,027 primary buildings, only 4,453 or 56 percent are suitable for educational purposes. 907 (11 percent) need to be pulled down, while the remaining 2,667 buildings need basic repairs.

6) 1,903 or 24 percent of the primary school buildings need sanitary utilities, 560 require sources of potable water, and 4,837 (60 percent) need electricity.

7) 1,970 schools operate only in the afternoon and 1,972 schools are on double shift.

8) Failures in the second and fourth grades are about 15 percent in each grade. Drop-outs for the total primary school are about 20 percent The loss and wastage of failures and drop-outs are evaluated at 27 million pounds a year.

"As shown in each and every one of these cases, none of the allocated sums would really meet the pupils' requirements for this important stage of popular education." (Specialized National Council Magazine, 1982, pp62-64).

The Specialized National Council on Education also surveyed the preparatory schools. The curriculum was unified with some courses in technical education, home economics, and agriculture for a total of 32 periods a week. There were approximately 150 modern preparatory schools emphasizing practical skills. "Education in such schools was supposed to depend on practical work alongside theoretical culture, but as a result of overcrowding, workshops and amenities that were transformed into classrooms, the teaching of practical subjects is done in an imaginary sort of way and does not realize the object of founding such schools." (Kotb, 1976, p.27). Education in the preparatory stage concentrated on preparing students for the preparatory examination in a number of theoretical subjects. Further, there existed a quantitative and qualitative shortage of staff. Most of the available teachers were educationally unqualified. In-service training provided by the ministry has been considered a failure due to the "limited proficiency" of the instructors and the necessarily short length of the training period. (Kotb, 1976, p.28).

Preparatory school buildings were in no better condition than those of the primary schools. Overcrowding increased the density of students in the classrooms and new classrooms had been built on the playgrounds using every available inch of space. Some buildings not originally intended as schools had to be used, and they lacked resources. Libraries were in need of modern books. In both primary and preparatory schools there was a concerted effort to implement compulsory education with a myriad of problems resulting from this effort.

The population explosion was the most obvious factor undermining Egypt's ability to provide adequate elementary and preparatory education. The 1966 census showed an annual growth rate of 2.54 percent, one of the highest in the world. By the 1970's, children born in the 1960's were ready to enter schools, causing increases in pupil-teacher and pupil-classroom ratios. (Helmy, 1979, p.6). Primary schools enrolled 75 percent of the 6 year olds in 1979, as compared to 46 percent in 1959. (Boktor, 1979, p. 7). This enrollment increase was achieved in spite of the growth in the number of 6 year-olds during that period. Preparatory schools also increased in student enrollment. In 1963, they enrolled 20 percent of the primary school graduates. By 1979, 50 percent of the primary school graduates were enrolled in preparatory schools. From 1978 to 1979, 200,000 additional students were enrolled, but the increase in population still kept the enrollment percentage at 50 percent for both years. (Boktor,

1979, p.7).
Women's educational level significantly
contributed to the population explosion. In a
society where women are economically dependent upon
men, illiteracy further compounds reliance upon men
for guidance and security. 1983 estimates of
illiteracy among women in some governorates (Assuit,
Fayoom) run as high as 90 percent compared to the
national average of 71 percent. (Schwartz, 1983,
interview). To some illiterate women, a feasible way
of keeping a husband is to have children. The more
children a women has, the less likely her husband is
to divorce her or take a second or third wife.
According to Islamic law, not having children is a
valid cause for divorce. The women, responding to
these conditions, have an average of 5.5 children.
This high fertility average coupled with a reduction
in the infant and child mortality rates has produced
a population of which 42 percent is under the age of
15. Thus, for every 100 adults between the ages of
16 and 65, there are approximately 78 dependent
children to be supported, reared, and educated. If
the present fertility average continues, the
population will double in the next 20 years,
resulting in an even larger school-age population.
(U.N. Fund for Population Activities, 1981, pp8-10).
Thus, the economic and social survival needs of the
illiterate woman support the population increase,
which in turn limits the children's educational
opportunities.

If the woman is educated, her training does not
contradict the importance of having children, as
education for women has historically reinforced
domesticity. Ain Shams Faculty for Girls has four
colleges - Science, Education, Arts, and Home
Economics; while Al-Azhar College for Girls adds
Religion and Languages to the offerings. The
American University in Cairo, a private institution
with 66 percent female enrollment, primarily
graduates students in mass communications and
economics. Still only 3 percent of the women ever
get a university education, even though it is free
through the doctorate. Egyptians view education for
women as a stopgap until they marry, and many women
once trained find little social encouragement from
parents, spouses or peers to work outside their
home. As a result, women, both literate and
illiterate, learn that their function is to marry
and have children, which further fuels the
population explosion.

Furthermore, economics limited the quality of

primary and preparatory education. Although L.E.20 of the L.E.28 allocated for the primary school child goes for wages, teachers' salaries are inadequate considering inflation increases despite government subsidies of food, fuel, and transportation. For example, between 1960 and 1965, the price of eggs per unit increased 133.3 percent, meat 150 percent, and sugar 185.7 percent. (Wahba, 1977, p.12). The official inflation rate was estimated by the World Bank to be 30 percent in 1983. (Snaith, 1983, interview) Thus, teachers have a strong economic incentive to seek outside employment. The shortened school day enables them to have second jobs or tutor their students after class. Some teachers have been accused of providing unclear or incomplete classroom instuction in order to insure a student's need of tutoring to succeed on exams. Others might accept favors in order to raise test scores. While all of these accusations are difficult to verify, the enormous amount of family income and energy expended to get children tutored is evident. "The overspreading phenomenon of private lessons whether in schools or universities has become one of the major drawbacks in the education system," Dr. Mustafa Kamal Helmi, Minister of Education, said in 1983 in an interview with <<Musawar>> magazine. "Fixed monthly wages for tutors are currently allocated from the budget of each family especially for general certificate exams. Since private lessons are a burden to the parents who are taxpayers, the government should find solutions to this problem in order to serve the citizens in the best possible way, since this is the true meaning for socialism and democracy."

Much of the instruction does take place outside the classroom. If economically feasible, tutors are hired, thus supplementing teaching salaries. If not feasible, children do the best they can in overcrowded facilities which lack reference materials, equipment, laboratories, and trained teachers. Without the understanding these resources provide, the students memorize the textbooks in order to pass exams. Many are unable to pass, to endure overcrowded conditions, or, in short, to cope. These become the primary and preparatory drop-outs, and these failures added to the number of children who never enroll, comprise a large population of illiterate children.

Tables 7,8, and 9 show the number of students enrolled in grade 1, and the number of successes in 6th grade final exam. The calculation of the gross value of primary education productivity is taken per 1000 students with the wastage in primary education as a result of deaths and failure.

TABLE 7

Total Primary School Wastage

Year	No enrolled in G 1	Wastage in Primary Education
70/71	742,888	42.3
71/72	722,193	41.2
72/73	727,273	41.8
73/74	578,322	34.1

TABLE 8

Number of drop-out boys from each of the six grades in primary education.

Year	G.1	G.2	G.3	G.4	G.5	G.6
70/71	10,250	8,530	15,130	23,590	16,610	38,500
71/72	10,200	2,720	14,880	14,800	18,180	35,090
72/73	8,780	8,930	12,430	23,310	14,600	25,390
73/74	4,580	6,400	10,410	24,300	13,760	15,170
74/75	7,390	9,320	5,640	21,710	22,560	25,650
75/76	4,670	12,170	9,630	20,030	27,110	7,650
76/77	11,880	7,220	10,000	17,700	35,310	23,450
77/78	11,270	11,340	11,190	19,620	40,210	23,290
78/79	11,550	11,660	12,100	20,080	48,500	18,360

TABLE 9

Number of drop-out girls from each of the six
grades in primary education.

Year	G.1	G.2	G.3	G.4	G.5	G.6
70/71	14,450	11,700	16,470	23,840	14,300	24,230
71/72	14,580	13,360	17,440	23,390	14,340	22,640
72/73	12,160	10,720	14,160	20,550	11,400	15,830
73/74	7,860	4,470	12,290	21,870	11,550	13,070
74/75	15,780	7,540	7,860	18,070	17,000	14,270
75/76	13,190	12,040	10,020	16,080	17,080	6,940
76/77	16,090	9,970	9,160	12,900	20,760	13,170
77/78	18,650	8,850	10,340	14,000	27,620	13,510
78/79	19,380	9,650	10,880	15,180	33,300	10,150

Furthermore, those who never enroll are more likely to be female and to live in rural areas. Throughout primary, preparatory, and secondary education, the ratio of male to female enrollment is 60-40. (Ministry of Education, 1980, pp2-31). The resulting national illiteracy for females is 71 percent compared to 42 percent for males. School enrollment and drop-out figures do not reflect the geographic distribution. Forty-five percent of the total population live in urban areas where 90 percent of the elementary age children are initially enrolled in school. Fifty-five percent of the population live in rural areas where 69 percent of the elementary age population are initially enrolled in primary school.

From 1970 into the 1980's, enrollment was increased in elementary and preparatory education, greatly restricting the education provided. In the primary schools, increased class size combined with shortened school days reduced the amount of instruction that could be given. Teaching salaries which averaged L.E.50-60 a month did not attract quality teachers or motivate them to spend time on preparation. These were the conditions that existed for those who were able to enroll, attend, or pass exams. The failures, drop-outs, or those who never enrolled were not a part of the compulsory education system.

61

Expanding enrollment in secondary schools likewise resulted in severe problems with technical graduates, manpower shortages in critical technical areas, wastage, and the disillusionment of graduates.

Technical educational expansion was still crucial for the development of the country but the admission process discouraged talented students from selecting it. For the 60 percent of the preparatory school students who continued their secondary education, numerous technological educational avenues were open to them, based upon their scores on the final preparatory exam, personal preferences, and spaces available. Those with the highest scores (44 percent) attend general secondary school. The second highest group attend commercial, industrial, or agricultural high schools (53 percent). The lowest graduates (3 percent) go to teacher training institutes. (Kotb, 1976, p.29).

> It could be also said generally that education in the first form in the present secondary general is characterized by its verbosity and the attention it gives to theoretical studies without very much care to understanding or to acquiring mental, practical, or conductive aptitudes which develop personality and help in the integrated buildup of the pupils. (El Koussy, 1978, p.43).

Those who succeed in entering secondary schools (60,000) might be admitted into nursing/technical secondary schools or non-formal technical programs in the Ministries of Defense and Industry. These non-formal schools may provide training in such areas as weaving, carpentry, or welding. The training may vary from a few weeks to two years, depending on the complexity of the skill. Enrollment figures are not available on these non-formal schools, as they may be administered by agencies other than the Ministry of Education. (Nowier, 1983, interview). One obvious effect of the secondary selection process has been that the elite will attend general rather than technical or non-formal secondary schools. In addition to being a source of status and pride to oneself and family, success within the formal secondary system guarantees government employment.

Employment for all careers is determined by

exams which are critical social and educational
obstacles for the students. National exams are the
only feasible way to maintain objective standards
for the millions of students who want to continue
their free education. Test-taking skills often
supersede learning how to apply knowledge, becoming
the focus of instruction at all levels, particularly
on the secondary exam (thanaweyya 'ama). But test
scores do not necessarily measure competency or
understanding -- especially in technical areas where
application is a critical aspect of the content.
Test scores have, however, provided a cut-off
measure for those who are eligible for the security
and status of a government position.

> The people have become used to the
> prevailing patterns of exams, just
> as they have become used to the
> notion of education merely as a means
> for obtaining a certificate which
> would lead to a job, a job which is
> associated with a specific
> certificate and preceded by a
> specific number of years in education
> which would mean a specific salary
> and a specific place on the social
> ladder. If, however, the job was
> connected with a different
> certificate, preceded by a different
> number of years, it would mean a
> different salary and a different
> place on the social ladder. People
> have become attached to these
> prevailing conditions. They suffer
> and complain, and yet they have
> become so conditioned to this
> suffering that they find it hard to
> rid themselves of it." (El Koussy,
> 1978, p.43).

> Reliance on the exams, the "a'dadeya"
> and the "thanaweyya 'ama", to
> determine students' educational
> potential has resulted in uneven
> access to educational opportunities,
> affecting both the teachers' and
> students' economic status. Prior to
> these critical exams, extensive
> tutoring by private teachers has
> become the norm for families who can
> afford the expensive investment.

> Children from poorer families do not
> receive this intensive one-on-one
> preparation and are therefore clearly
> less likely to achieve high marks on
> the exams -- tests that will, to a
> large extent, determine the future
> courses of their lives. (Katz, 1983).

The status of a high score on the thanaweyya
'ama exam enables one to go to medical school, one
of the most prestigious of occupations even with a
beginning government salary of L.E.70 per month. If
one can afford to establish a clinic, he/she can,
perhaps, after a couple of years, make as much as a
plumber in the private sector. The Ministry of
Education understands the importance of the status
the people place on theoretical education. In a
speech given to the People's Assembly, the Minister
of Education said,

> The ministry is exerting effort to
> try and gap the difference in the
> view the people take of general
> secondary education as being the
> socially higher and the technical as
> being inferior and this by way of
> including some technical subjects in
> the general secondary education and
> by increasing the weight and raising
> the level of cultural subjects in
> technical schools and again by
> opening doors and entrances to
> technical school leavers... the
> ministry firmly believes that the
> ideal solution is the adoption of the
> inclusive school so that it would be
> possible to combine the theoretical,
> the scientific, the technical, and
> the technological, all in one frame.
> (Helmy, 1977, p.17).

Technical education, therefore, usually begins
with the weaker student who receives instruction
from a less qualified instructor, reflecting an
acute shortage of technical and vocational
instructors. The social status defined in the
selection process places academic above technical
education. And free education encourages those who
can continue to do so despite employment in
vocational or technical fields which do not require
university education. For example, the butcher will

have a degree in economics, the taxi driver will have a degree in engineering. One can earn more money as a taxi driver or butcher in the private sector, but social status is enhanced by having an academic degree. It is neither prestigious nor economically rewarding to have a technical degree or a teaching diploma. As a result, the technical student is not likely to receive as effective instruction as the academic student. Further, many technical schools cannot afford the equipment or space necessary to provide practical training. Overcrowding in preparatory schools limit prerequisite practical experience. These conditions foster technical education based upon memorization of the textbook, the same process utilized in the academic secondary schools. Such training does not aid the technical student in solving problems on the job and he may find difficulty in producing, and aiding in the country's development.

Technological education must also prepare for the extreme shortage of manpower in critical areas of development. From 1971 to 1979, the number of graduates from three-year and newer five-year technical programs jumped from 56,000 to 120,000, while the graduates from commercial schools corresponded closely to the annual manpower needs and the industrial education graduates (35,000) constituted only half the estimated needs. Personnel for shipbuilding, petroleum production, naval and agricultural engineering, and hygiene have been in demand over the last decade, but as of 1979 no technical training programs have existed for these areas. (Katz, 1983, p.44).

The manpower shortage problem had been identified earlier. A National Council of Manpower and Training was established in 1976 to address the utilization of human resources, co-ordinate education with long-and short-range economic and social goals, and work toward reducing unemployment. The problem was not so much one of lack of manpower but rather one of lack of skilled workers in specific areas. A standing commission to study the manpower situation started to work in 1963. Since then, yearly reports and studies have been made.

In spite of all the studies, the Ministry of Education had a shortage of 20,000 teachers in 1975. (Hyde, 1978, p.49). At the same time, the Egyptian government alleviated the unemployment problem by spending L.E.16 million to provide jobs for 1974 university graduates and 1973 graduates of intermediate technical schools. (Hyde, 1978, p.50).

The lack of co-ordination between education and
manpower needs resulted in additional financial
expenditure for the government as all graduates were
guaranteed employment within two years after
graduation. (National Council Magazine, 1981, p.62).
In 1981, 23 percent of the primary school teachers
needed further training. (National Councils
Magazine, 1981, p.67). They held neither a diploma
in education from one of the teacher training
institutions nor from another source such as a
faculty of education at a university. The main
training centers for primary school teachers were in
the five-year teacher institutes which accepted
graduates of preparatory schools. (Helmy, 1982,
p.5). Only 1 percent of the primary school teachers
were university graduates. Though some 25 to 30
percent of the teachers in the primary and
preparatory schools had less than the desired
professional preparation, there were no "para-
professionals" employed as such. (Ministry of
Education, 1979, p.52). The manpower shortage of
skilled teachers and vocational and technical
workers could not be quickly addressed within the
centralized educational system.

> The Egyptian government has recently
> reaffirmed its commitment to
> providing public sector jobs to all
> graduates of technical secondary
> schools, post-secondary institutes
> and universities, insuring that
> increasing numbers of students will
> choose these academic routes. But
> because government jobs are assured,
> there is little impetus from students
> of academic institutions to introduce
> much-needed technical and practical
> training into their education. If the
> government guarantee was lifted,
> students would be more likely to seek
> skills marketable in the private
> sector. The government could
> eliminate large numbers of redundant
> personnel in its swollen ministries,
> and instead select government workers
> by merit, improving the quality and
> efficiency of its work. However, the
> job guarantee, combined with a
> general attitude that manual work is
> inferior, insures that most students
> will continue to choose the non-

technical educational tracks. (Katz, 1983, p.44).

Egypt's future development is dependent upon the skills of technicians, skilled laborers, and innovative problem solvers. The educational system has produced a high percentage of graduates in fields such as medicine, engineering, architecture and law. Even in technical schools, the emphasis of education was on the theoretical rather than the practical--a result of borrowing needed technical instructors from higher institutes and a lack of equipment for practical training. Egyptian commercial and industrial expansion has been hampered by the lack of adequately trained personnel while theoretically trained university graduates are underemployed. This assessment was clearly made by the National Council for Education, Scientific Research and Technology.

> The assessment of the prevailing situation in the institutes and schools of technical education points to a number of basic observations, the most prominent of which is that of the large percentage of drop-outs among students enrolled in technical institutes. In general, it was observed that few students are interested in industrial education and there is a shortage in the number of new institutes for training technicians and for agricultural education. Again, there are short-comings in the upgrading and diversification of these institutes in a manner that would enable them to cope with the needs and economic development of modern times. The assessment also showed the necessity of reinforcing various aspects of the teaching operation in technical education. (Higher Education Outside the Universities, 1980, p.56).

Aside from the low social status attached to technical labor, Egyptian society has not provided experience and exposure to technical training. Technicians historically have been imported Europeans or Russians. As an agrarian society with a surplus of manpower, mechanization has meant

unemployment for Egyptian workers. In a country
where few people own cars much less tractors,
knowledge of how to build vehicles or even the
utilization of such technology as complicated as
internal combustion engines are not common in the
society. To then select training in mechanical or
agricultural technology is not an obvious choice to
the young Egyptian. Further, because jobs are
assured, there is little motivation for students at
academic institutions to introduce much practical
training into their education. And as technical
education is determined by so many different
government agencies, long-range planning and
responding to critical needs require co-ordination
between educational and manpower agencies, a
difficult, time-consuming task. For example, one
school, established in 1980-1981 to train
agricultural technicians, had yet to graduate
students in 1984-reflecting the long periods
involved in responding to emerging needs once
identified.

Technical and vocational needs had been
identified and reports written, but the necessarily
slow implementation of changes contributed to the
third major educational problem of the 1980's,
wastage. Wastage is found in many aspects of the
system. Enrollment increased at all levels and the
drop-out rate has been reduced, but drop-out figures
continued to reveal 18 percent of primary students
did not pass the exit exam, and 68 percent of
preparatory students could not be placed in
secondary schools. The exams and difficulties in
attending school, particularily in rural areas,
resulted in 30-48 percent of the students dropping
out of elementary school. (Basic Education Report,
1979, p.167). These drop-outs, added to the
approximately 20 percent of the students nationally
who never enroll, comprised a number of students not
currently in primary school. The enrollment drops
drastically after primary school. In 1980-1981, 4.5
million children were enrolled in primary school.
Approximately 1.5 million were enrolled in
preparatory school and approximately 1 million in
secondary education. These drop-outs, added to the
numbers that never enrolled, indicated a population
which continued to exist with meager skills and/or
illiteracy.

And, finally, there is the wastage and
disillusionment of some graduates. Those who would
like to be engineers do not get high enough marks
and must go to commercial schools, or do not

continue their education. The government positions which are guaranteed sometimes are awarded two years after graduation and pay poorly or are unnecessary. The graduate finds he is paid little and/or is unneeded, and becomes angry. Perhaps the greatest disadvantage of the current system is the loss of work performance from disenchanted graduates-- graduates waiting for jobs that befit their status, graduates trying to learn occupations for which they have no training, or graduates who are trained in agriculture, for example, but would rather be public relations officers. Most significant are the graduates who work abroad where they earn more money but must leave behind family and friends for years in countries, many of which view them as second class citizens. It is the unfortunate situation that workers in the technical and professional areas that Egypt needs desperately are also useful in other developing countries that do not have a socialized economy. Doctors, teachers, engineers, and technologists earn as much as 10 times the Egyptian salary in other Arab-speaking countries. For those who graduate and accept secure government postions, disenchantment also results in a negative work environment and low productivity.

The "educated" are the elite in the society and desire respect. Those who have been trained in higher status jobs for which there is no employment regardless of their actual competencies, sometimes have little interest in jobs which have lower status. Vast employment opportunities exist for vital jobs such as plumbers, carpenters, and electricians, but "educated" persons would not consider doing manual labor. Or, as educated people become taxi drivers and waiters, the work is viewed as temporary and filled accordingly. Rather than producing a well-trained labor force capable of meeting development needs, the educational process encourages avoidance of employment in areas not "suitable" in status. An enormous amount of Egyptian revenue is spent to produce graduates who cannot or will not meet the developmental needs of the country. Add to these the large number of men who have spent portions of their lives in the military and Egypt's current peacetime stability is threatened.

The Egyptian Gazette described the disillusionment and wastage in an article published in March of 1983.

A soresight to the downtown stroller

on a weekday morning is the vast army
of able-bodied men on the streets. A
visitor would assume they were
unemployed, but we know better. They
are, in large part, government
officials who have too little to do,
so they leave their offices on any
small pretext and go shopping, or
just walk around. One could say they
were unemployed, in a sense. The fact
is the government still guarantees to
employ every Egyptian graduate, and
lives up to its promises. This has
existed for so long--dating to the
reign of Abdul-Nasser--that it has
become virtually a national
tradition. Even posessors of the
school-leaving certificate are
guaranteed some sort of job. They
accept the meager pay for the
security, and the government accepts
their poor output and the fact that
most of them hardly have any work to
do, rather than have dole-queues.
Some people call this "masked
unemployment," and in its defence we
must say it at least spares the
humiliation and degradation of the
dole-queue.

However, if we take a look at the
type of people who go in for
government jobs in Egypt, we find
nearly all of them have one thing in
common. They are not very
adventurous, preferring security and
a pittance to the chance of earning
more money where there is an element
of risk. Worse still, most of them
are, psychologically or because of
the system, unable to work really
hard or to shoulder responsibility.
Decision making is completely beyond
them, hence the abundance of red tape
which, in the long run, means
everybody passing the buck. Of course
there are a few exceptions. The
Passport Department officials are
hard-working and employees of a
number of public sector
establishments are hard-working and

> occasionally have to make decisions.
> But they are in the minority. The
> whole government officials would
> appear to be unfit for anything other
> than a humdrum, mechanical sinecure
> where the routine never differs, year
> in and year out. (Government
> Workers, Egyptian Gazette, March
> 1983).

The reponsibility then, for Egypt's development rests not with the technical education but with the universities. Between 1970 and 1979, regional universities were opened in Mansura, Tanta, El Zagazig, Helwan (technical), Menia, Monofia, and Suez. Four hundred thousand university students were enrolled in 1976-77. By 1980, Ain Shams and Cairo University had combined enrollments of approximately 250,000. All education was free through the doctoral level, and until 1978 Nasser's policy of providing free education to Arab and African students who qualified was in effect. In 1983, the benefit of opening more universities without adequate staff, faculties, or facilities was examined as the university at Minofia existed only on paper. Resources for the university were not available.

The functioning of universities that are understaffed and overcrowded has resulted in situations which meet the economic survival needs of faculty and students, but not necessarily the educational requirements of the country. If a student desires to attend classes, sometimes as large as 5,000 in a lecture, he must fight for space. If he does not want to attend classes, he can buy the professor's lecture notes, the text, and only appear for the end-of-year exams which are constructed and graded by groups of professors and therefore must come from the text. Obviously there is not enough space for all the students to attend classes. When exams are given, tents are constructed in open campus areas in order to accommodate students. This system enables a student to have a full-time job while enrolled as a full-time student. Others may take extended vacations and pay friends to sign attendance sheets for them.

The professor, on the other hand, may be assigned to a university which may not be near where his family lives. As housing shortages are acute, he remains in his earlier location and commutes to his assignment. Because their salaries are low, some professors teach at two or three different universities, commuting on unreliable trains, poor roads, or through congested traffic. They may not arrive for their classes, making the printing and selling of lecture notes an economic and educational necessity. Without the benefit of a desks, secretaries, or class space, professors find their jobs so frustrating that they search for jobs outside Egypt where they can earn much more. The professors will, if possible, leave for these teaching assignments whenever they become available.

If interested in research, both the students and faculty encounter difficulties in overcrowded Egyptian universities. The library at Ain Shams Faculty of Education was closed from 1978 to 1980 when it was discovered bugs had eaten the books. As the only recourse, committed professors develop their own libraries which are then loaned to graduate students. Economics and the unavailability of reference resources, often restrict research capabilities of graduate students. As described by Szyliowicz (1973), incentives for scientific research are limited.

> Confronted with inadequate facilities, a lack of recognition and support, heavy teaching loads, misemployment of skills, mediocre colleagues, uninterested superiors, and intellectual isolation, the able young scientist finds it extremely difficult to engage in productive research. (p.19).

Awareness of these difficulties has necessitated that post-graduate students be trained abroad. But this system also has its pitfalls. There is the refusal of some post-graduate students to return home, the incompatibility of certain studies with Egyptian requirements, the great difference in the scientific levels between one country and another, and the length of the preparatory stage in certain cases (National Council Magazine, 1977, p.17). The recourse is to strengthen the universities, staffing and facilities, and then alter educational processes - a difficult task given the enormous number of people involved.

The difficulties of education in the 1970's were assessed in an article entitled, "The Need for Change" by Dr. Abdel Aziz El Koussy (1978):

> Some of the outstanding hindrances are limited financial resources for

the construction of suitable buildings with the required facilities, as
well as the appointment of needed
teachers. Another obstruction is the
population growth and their crowding
in such a way that does not allow for
the existence of necessary space
required for essential services. The
growth of the general awareness of
the need for education, and,
therefore, the demand for it, is
another factor. What is more, it
appears that although the necessary
policies, plans, and goals are
formulated on highly efficient
levels, the execution and performance
are not carried out with the same
degree of efficiency and in all
cases, an apparent gap between
planning and performance is clear...A
strong resistance to change is
prevailing for it seems people have
become accustomed to the existing
patterns which in turn have become an
indispensable part of their daily
life...Our pupils are brought up on
superficial, veneering selfishness
and committing things to memory
without comprehension, instead of
being brought up as individuals--
sociable and creative. We complain
that despite the small percentage of
the educated compared to the entire
population, the labor market in its
higher stratum is unable to absorb
the graduates, whether on quantitative qualitative, or assorted lines.
All this in addition to the scarcity
in the middle labor market of
professional labourers... All these
are different examples of the
existing imbalance. This imbalance
persists despite the fact that its
problems have been examined and
looked upside-down to such an extent
that we felt we were going in
circles, examining and re-examining
the same problems using the same
technique over and over again.
(p.45).

The educational conflict of the 1970's and 1980's reflected dichotomies between the rich and poor, Egyptian and foreign, government and secular interests. The problems were more acute than during Nasser's regime as the population had increased and school enrollment expanded. Wars and subsidies continued further depleting the country's resources. The government was unable to sustain the population and improve the quality of education. The dissatisfaction of students with the results of their educational efforts encouraged a resurgence of patriotic religious fundamentalism on one hand the the vigourous solicitation of foreign funds on the other. Either action was viewed as a means of addressing the collapsing economic and social environment. In 1981, the Moslem Brotherhood took action against the escalating foreign influence represented by Sadat. Had the accomplishments of the open door policy been as universally experienced as the inadequacies, the Muslim Brotherhood might not have felt the need to take matters into their own hands.

CHAPTER V REFERENCES

Boktor, Amir. (1979, November). "The Development and Expansion of Education in the United Arab Republic," Cairo, ARE, Ministry of Education.

El Koussy, Abdel Azzis. (1979). "The Need for Change," The Special National Councils Magazine, Presidency of the Republic, ARE.

Helmy, Mustafa Kamal, Minister of Education. (1983, February). "Time to Check Widespread Private Lessons," Egyptian Gazette, Cairo, ARE.

Helmy, Mustafa Kamal, Minister of Education. (1979, November). "Perspectives in Education in Modern Egypt," Cairo, ARE.

Helmy, Mustafa Kamal, Minister of Education. (1977, June). "University Post-Graduate Studies," The Specialized National Councils Magazine, Cairo, ARE.

Human Resources Management, Inc. (1979, August). "Basic Education in Egypt, Report of the Joint Egyptian-American Survey Team," Cairo, ARE.

The International Journal of Middle East Studies. "The Future Economic Integration within the Arab World."

Kotb, Yousef. (1976). "On the Development of General Secondary Education, Its Objectives, Plans of Study, Syllabuses, Branching Off System, and Choice of Subjects in the General Secondary Education Examination Certificate," The Specialized National Councils Magazine, Presidency of the Republic, ARE.

Maddy-Weitzman, Bruce. (1981, Summer, Vol. 25, No. 2). "The Fragmentation of Arab Politics: Inter-Arab Affairs Since the Afghanistan Invasion," Orbis.

Ministry of Education, General Department of Statistics. (1981). "Annual Atatistics, 1980-81," Cairo, ARE.

Ministry of Education. (1979, September). "Working Paper on Developing and Innovating Education in Egypt," Cairo, ARE.

Ministry of Education. (1982, July). "Working Paper on Developing and Innovating Education in Egypt," Cairo, ARE.

Nowier, Gammal, consultant for the National Center for Educational Research. (1983, July). Personal interview.

Pierre, Andrew. (1978, Summer, Vol. 3, No. 1). "Beyond the 'Plane Package,' Arms and Politics in the Middle East," International Security.

Schwartz, Dr. Karl, educational consultant for USAID. (1983, March). Personal interview.

Snaith, Andy, finance officer, American University in Cairo. (1983, March). Speech to the University Budget Committee, American University in in Cairo, Cairo, ARE.

The Specialized National Councils Magazine, Presidency of the Republic. (1981). "Economics of the Educational Costs of the Primary Stage," Cairo, ARE.

Springboard, Robert. (1981, Winter, Vol. 24, No. 4). "U.S. Policy Toward Egypt: Problems and Prospects." Orbis, A Journal of World Affairs.

Szyliowicz, Joseph S. "Education and Modernization in the Middle East," Cornell University Press, 1973.

United Nations Fund for Population Activities. (1981, January, Report No.3). "Arab Republic of Egypt, Report of Mission on Needs Assessment and Population Assistance," New York, New York.

Wahab, Salah Abdel. (1977). "Inflation: Causes and Remedies for Inflation in Egypt," The Specialized National Councils Magazine, Cairo, ARE.

CHAPTER VI

REORGANIZATION OF MASS EDUCATION

1970's - 1980's

        History has set in motion two separate
educational movements, the "open door" foreign
investment in educational projects and programs and
the Egyptian populist, reorganization of education.
For the most part, the foreign movement directed
itself toward the elite while the Egyptian
reorganization directed itself toward the masses.
The goals of Egyptian populist reform were clearly
delineated in 1979 when the Ministry of Education
prepared a "Working Paper of Development and
Innovations of Egyptian Education." This paper was
submitted for review to all the popular and
political bodies, the trade unions, universities,
local authorities, cultural and economic experts,
and everyone concerned with education and its
reform. The Ministry of Education then reviewed
reports from all groups and integrated them into a
comprehensive report entitled "Developing and
Innovating Education in Egypt--Policy, Plans and
Implementation Programs." The concepts about reform
represented a comprehensive national action, the
basic principles of which were sanctioned by the
National Democratic Party Congress, approved by the
Ministerial Committee on Services and by the
executive cabinet in the November 2, 1980, session.
The implementation began in 1981 to continue for
five years as a joint responsibility of educational
and governmental systems. In other words, the
populist movement had the sanction of all power
centers in the government and in the socialistic
private sector. As can be noted in the following
accounts of accomplishments as obtained from top
ministry officials, expanding enrollment and
reducing illiteracy continue as the primary goals of
the educational reorganization plan.

In 1981, the legislature passed Law 139, comprehensive educational legislation. The priorities of the reorganization plan which are supported by legislation have made significant progress without substantial foreign investment. The accomplishments through 1983-84 have been confirmed through interviews with Ministry of Education officials.

The following principles were determined to direct the process of educational development--for deepening the roots of democracy, for comprehensive development and productive work in the context of cultural identity, and for a lifelong process. It was agreed to implement this educational reform as a multi-targeted, multi-dimensional strategy. All of these goals were to be achieved via several major and minor programs which jointly aimed to meet the principles of the new educational policy.

1. Expansion of pre-school child education.

The ultimate goal of this project is to provide increasing educational opportunities for pre-school children. Implementation of this program was scheduled to start as of the school-year 1980-1981.

First, there has been an expansion of the number of pre-schools affiliated with primary schools. In 1983-1984, 300 new classes were begun. Governorates were asked to expand pre-school education in order to aid working mothers. Further, in July 1978, the Ministry of Education started an Experimental Language School project by establishing 12 such schools. By 1981, forty schools existed. English language is introduced at the pre-primary stage in spite of the limited resources of the ministry and the shortage of trained teachers. "There have been many difficulties, problems and complaints from the parents of children in the pre-primary stage in these schools." (Yacoub, 1982, p. 2). The result has been a modification of the teacher training curricula for primary teachers to include English courses. (Khalil, Y., personal interview, May 1983).

The basis for the expansion and the specifications of location, buildings, capacity, utilities, equipment and sanitary requirements, school system, curricula, plans admission prerequests, staffing for supervision and teaching as well as cost for attendance are legislated in Law 139 of 1981, Article 8. All responsibility and power for the establishment of new pre-school is rested in the Ministry of Education.

2. Basic education development.

Recognizing the deficiencies of the present primary and preparatory educational system, the Egyptian government reorganized and combined the first nine years of education into what was called Basic Education. The goals were to prevent a "backsliding into illiteracy and meaningful participation in practical life." It would also become a complete stage in itself, enabling its graduates to contribute to the various economic and social activities of their environment, pushing these activities towards progress and development. The pupil should be prepared for practical life within his own environment by bringing him to a standard of growth that would help him forge his working life, whether agricultural, industrial, or commercial, by providing him with the necessary training. It must also prepare some graduates for advanced studies. Compulsory education was extended to 15 rather than 12 years. The program for National Action issued in 1971 stipulated that Basic Education should be expanded by 1980 to absorb all those of obligatory age.

By 1983, the problem of facilities, teachers, equipment, increasing enrollment, and curriculum for Basic Education had been addressed. In 1981, the Ministry of Education allocated L.E.300 to every primary school for equipment. Every classroom in 5th and 6th grades were allocated L.E.40 and every preparatory classroom received L.E.60 for raw materials. This allocation was made in addition to the L.E.10 million annual expenditure of the USAID for maps, globes, and other instructional materials. UNICEF provided $1 million in 1980 and the U.S. expenditure which began in 1981 was to continue until 1985.

Basic education is one of the few projects obtaining foreign funding concerned with the elementary age child. USAID allocated $39 million for new Basic Education buildings and classrooms in five governorates based upon a school mapping assessment. The mapping identified geographic areas where schools could be built within walking distance for a large number of children. The Ministry of Education allocated L.E.70 million over five years beginning in 1983 to be spent for new schools, additional workshops, and building repair.

The curriculum added practical training

beginning in 1978 with 450 experimental schools. In 1980-81, all primary schools became Basic Education schools with the 7th grade to be added in 1982-83, 8th in 1983-84, and 9th in 1984-85.

Syllabuses were prepared in social sciences but not implemented because decisions had not been made regarding the textbooks. Cassel, MacMillan, Longman and Hineman publishers spent one year preparing books after visiting schools and piloting material. Each publisher supplied the ministry with a limited number of sample books.

Primary and preparatory schools were combined into 9 years of Basic Education in 1982-83. This combination was preceded by a National Conference on Basic Education conducted for teachers, school administrators and concerned persons in 1980-81. (Chairman, Basic Education Program, personal interview, 1983).

USAID supported Basic Education outputs will include 6,595 new classrooms 1,000 schools and approximately 140 person months of technical assistance and related activities. The grant covers 60 percent of the primary and preparatory schools and will be combined with L.E.70 million the Egyptian Ministry of Education will spend on buildings schools and equipment. The Academy for Educational Development initially funded at L.E.2 million began a four-stage project consisting of the establishment of advisory committees, needs assessments conducted by technical experts in all project areas, a computerized plan to collect data from the needs assessments and discussions of the results. Approval for approximately 200 Americans to spend 4 or 5 months rebuilding curricula was obtained and began in 1984. (Schwartz, K., personal interview, April 1983). Another USAID grant was awarded to Creative Services, an American academy to evaluate the expenditure of the USAID grant for classroom materials. Negotiations with the Egyptian officials began in March and April of 1983 but were not conclusive. (Creative Services Consultant, personal interview, April 1983).

3. Secondary education development.

The ultimate aim of the general secondary education development program was the up-grading of the efficiency of general secondary education, development of its programs, curricula and evaluation techniques as well as infusing it with certain vocational training skills. Implementation was to extend though the middle of the 80's.

Chapter 3 of Law 139 of 1981 concerned length of study, reputation, exams requirements, and dismissal in secondary education. Curricula and the content of exams were to be defined by decrees of the Ministry of Education with the approval of the Higher Council of Education. Study was to include "major subjects for all students and optional subjects to be chosen from according to the students' aptitudes and abilities." (Law 139, 1981, p. 4).

A new curriculum extending basic education curricula was written. The focus was on practical activities to not only enable the graduate to join a university but also to enable her/him to find work in technical areas. In order to increase the enrollment in technical secondary schools, the entrance requirements for general secondary education were raised in 1983-84.(Under-secretary Ministry of Education, personal interview, April 1983).

One school in Tanta and one in Sohag implemented a comprehensive secondary curriculum. These schools offered a number of compulsory subjects and a group of optional subjects within a flexible curriculum. They also offered one or two of the vocational areas which the students had been involved in through the Basic Education experiment. (Comprehensive School Report, 1980, p. 15).

4. Development of technical education.

Technical education aims at training a class of skilled workers in the 3-year technical schools and a class of technicians in the 5-year technical schools in commercial agricultural and industrial fields. Implementation started in the 1980-1981 school year.

In 1980-1981, objectives, courses and schedules were developed for 3 years and 5 years of commercial agricultural, industrial and technical schools. All were approved by the Ministry of Education, Labor and Industry. (Director, National Center for Educational Rearch, personal interview, May 1983).

5. Promoting education in regions of a special nature.

Educational expansion in regions of a special nature focused on one-classroom schools in "environments where illiteracy, poverty, and disease prevail" and areas such as the Sinai. In 1975-76, one-classroom schools were re-examined with the aim of providing elementary skills in reading, writing, Arabic, religion, social science, and science education in order to reduce poverty, illiteracy, and disease (These schools had increased in number, especially after the Israeli invasion in 1976 when Egyptian schools located in dangerous areas were relocated in safer villages and towns). At the end of the 1979-80 school year, the five-year experiment was evaluated regarding the success of the material, the level of student achievement, and the students enrolled. (World Bank, 1981, pp. 1-59).

The one-classroom schools were established in existing buildings with the bulk located in mosques. The academic year was that of the ministry with anywhere from 3 to 12 hours of instruction per week. Each classroom was among 50 assigned to an educational supervisor located at a mother school. Each of these conditions limited the effectiveness of the classroom. The activities of the mosque restricted the attendance of women and hours of usage--even though one-classroom schools might begin anytime between 8 a.m. and 2 p.m. Rural communication systems and roads made it difficult for supervisors to adequately monitor educational processes, especially with 50 remote classrooms assigned for visitation. Furthermore, the academic schedule was often incompatible with harvest periods when teachers and students were needed in the fields.

Secondly, the curricula were the same as that of the government primary schools. Six textbooks were needed for each of the six classes taught, contributing to educational confusion as the one-classroom school was conducted only half the length of time as the government primary schools. So while the curriculum was extensive, absences made keeping pace even more difficult. And absences were influenced by a number of factors--fieldwork, weather when there was no school roof, sickness, irregularity of teachers' attendance, inadequate clothing, and the fact that no meals were served. The excessive number of texts required for each course, the shortened school day, and increased absences made completion of coursework most difficult. The teachers hired for one-classroom schools all had second jobs.

In 1979-80, 30 percent of the teachers were qualified and waiting for placement in a school compatible with their qualifications. Fifty-seven percent had immediate qualifications and 22 percent had no qualifications and viewed teaching as a means of increasing income. All teachers were paid approximately 20 piasters per class and, with a maximum of 16 classes a week, they received a maximum of L.E.14 per month. It is obvious that the quality of instruction was affected by the amount of energy and competency of the teacher. In all areas of student learning, the better qualified teacher produced students with higher achievement levels.

The basic question was how much the students learned in one-classroom schools compared to formal schools. Based on special exams designed to evaluate one-classroom schools, learning in all subjects was measured. Arabic achievement was considered satisfactory and religious training superior to that of students in formal primary schools, revealing a similarity to kuttabs of the past. Seventy percent was a general average on the exam.

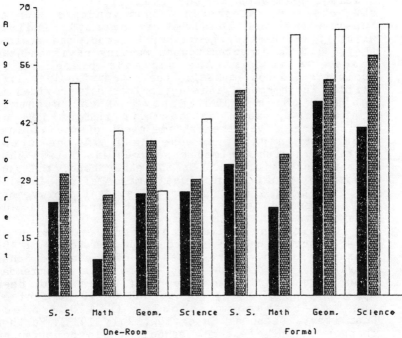

Comparison of One-Room and Formal Classrooms

First Three Cycles or Grades

The improved performance in the second and third cycles was attributed to the transfer of students from formal schools to one-classroom schools and drop-outs from the first cycle.

It seems apparent that students in one-classroom schools were acquiring some basic skills in reading, writing, mathematics, science, social science, and Arabic. Given the level of teaching competencies, the educational conditions, and the background of the students, the acquisition of knowledge was considered adequate. (World Bank, 1981, pp. 1-59).

However, the level and type of skills were not functional-- either in the village environment or within the academic context. Academically, the competency achieved was not high enough to allow the average student to pass the Primary School Exams, acquire a certificate, and continue his education, even if allowed to take the exam. Secondly, minimal skills were not integrated appropriately into village life and did not enable students to significantly affect the level of disease, illiteracy, and poverty in their environment. As briefly mentioned in the evaluation report, if subjects were integrated around concepts such as "up-grading the local environment," reading, writing, arithmetic, geometry, science, and ethics, they could be directed toward meeting environmental needs. As it was, the subjects presented in isolation did not emphasize their transfer into life skills. Furthermore, instruction was not provided in subjects which would improve local economic conditions, such as cottage industries or agriculture. Given the extreme needs of the village areas, transplanting one half of the urban curriculum with minimal resources was a less than satisfactory solution. On the other hand, the one-classroom school project was a major effort in size and variety of locations and the student achievement level was adequate, given the curriculum and constraints.

Despite the evaluation report, expansion of one-classroom schools has continued. A total of 151 classroom schools were added in Belharia and Sohag provinces. Implementation of curriculum recommendations in the World Bank report of 1980 has not been apparent. As of 1983, Fayoom had 60-70 percent of the one-classroom schools. (USAID Project Consultant, personal interview, July 1983). Further changes in one-classroom schools could be effected by the Minister of Education. He was empowered in

Law 139 of 1981 to establish experimental schools and to determine conditions and regulations of admission as well as examination systems. The goal of experimental schools is to allow field applications of educational experiments moving toward "generalization" (Article 9). While the number of one-classroom schools might prevent them from being considered experimental, there is enough flexibility in this legislation to allow experimentation for schools of a special nature.

Recent efforts to increase enrollment have been supported by Law 139 of 1981 which fines parents when children do not attend school. The 1983 enrollment figures estimate that 80 percent of 6-year olds are in school, but population increases, drop-outs, failures, and difficulties in attendance for females in certain geographical locations have counteracted the national effort to provide elementary numeracy and literacy for the elementary-age population.

The ultimate aim of this program is to offer up-to-date educational services in regions of a special nature (i.e. areas of land reclamation, Sinai and the northern coast.) Implementation took place in 1980-1981.

6. Consolidation of non-formal education.

This program aims at consolidating non-formal education. It includes local communities' development, vocational training, agricultural extension, labor, culture and public information, education of the young, education, and adult-oriented training programs whether pre-service and in-service programs or programs organized prior to initiation into a new job. Implementation started with the school year of 1980-1981. Non-formal education was more closely linked with formal education through the introduction of 4,500 one-classroom schools. These schools were conducted for those who had previous access to formal education. (Ministry of Education, Developing and Innovating Education in Egypt 1980-81).

7. Student educational welfare.

The ultimate aim is to establish religious and moral values, deepen the roots of democracy in the hearts of the young, and provide nutrition, health care and educational, vocational and psychological guidance as well as educational activities at an improved level.

Student educational welfare has mostly focused on nutrition and health care for eight million students in rural areas and some districts of Cairo and Alexandria. A meal a day basically consisting of bread was provided. A cooperative program between the Egyptian government the U.S.-sponsored Catholic Relief Association, World Bank, and initially the U.N., has been operating for eight years with the gradual reduction of U.S. and World Bank money toward the goal of Egypt eventually carrying all expenses of the program (Catholic Relief Officer, personal interview, March 1983).

8. Welfare of handicapped and distinguished students.

Education for the special and handicapped student is conducted in three settings, residential schools, classrooms adjacent to regular schools and hospitals. Every governorate has one or more special education schools. Special education for those with stays of three monthsor more in the hospital is provided either in classrooms in the hospital or by tutors who visit the hospital rooms. Classrooms for rheumatic and polio patients are located in hospitals and financed by the Ministry of Education.

The curriculum is especially adapted for the blind or partially sighted, deaf, or mentally retarded. Classes in most cases are no larger than six children. The need for special sensory training and the curricula adaptations have required that the years of compulsory education be extended from six to nine years for the blind and mentally retarded and from nine to eleven years for the deaf. The last three years of instruction in all schools prepare the students for vocational careers. Special instruction for the deaf is in lip reading and for the blind in speech, physical therapy and Braille. Textbooks are translated into Braille for the blind, and the deaf are aided with group and individual hearing aids, thermophones and audio-typing. The language of instruction is Arabic with English available in residential schools.

Teachers for the special and handicapped students are graduates of the teacher training institutes and have three years of teaching experience with an additional year of training at a special center at Abou Seya. More than 100 teachers are trained each year and they earn 30 percent higher salaries than regular teachers. The new plan for training has added psychology of handicapped, student teaching and observation. There is an interest in providing more instruction for the teachers in order to further raise their level of competency.

Schooling is provided for the mentally retarded. Educable students are selected from those with IQ's between 50 and 70 as determined in a psychological clinic in the Ministry of Health.

Further, two schools for delinquents in Cairo are providing psychological services, social care and education, one for boys in Giza and one for girls in Dokki. The minister of education has stated that he wants to give special education all the money they want and expansion planned for handicapped and special education indicates this is so. New classes will be added to increase the enrollment of 10,000 students enrolled in 1983.

9. Evaluation and Examinations techniques and systems.

The ultimate aim is the development of systems and techniques of evaluation and examinations. Objective testing and some problem-solving were added to the testing procedure. (Khalil, Y., personal interview). As of April 1983, $33,000 of L.E.50,000 USAID of the English Language Testing and Evaluation grant was not spent. The grant, which was to end February 28, 1982, was extended for training and equipment. Training consisted of a four-day workshop/seminar in testing for English language inspectors in 1982 and the establishment of a professional diploma scholarship program at American University in Cairo. Thirty Egyptians applied and four met A.U.C admission standards and were accepted. As of the spring of 1983, two students were enrolled. A micro-processor, printer and software were purchased to meet the training needs of the two diploma candidates. Further projected English Language Testing and Evaluation goals will be to continue the diploma scholarships program. (Henning, G., Mid-Term AID English Language Training Report, March 1983).

10. Up-grading the efficiency of the educational system through improving student inflow rates, rectification of private education and taking action to step up its level.

The ultimate aim has been to improve the

efficiency level of the educational system through increased student inflow rates, reform of private education and action to up-grade its level.

The goal of all educational reorganization has been to increase enrollment. The accomplishments are demonstrated in the expansion of primary, general secondary and technical education. The mandated fining of parents for students' failure to attend and the efforts to integrate non-formal education and education in regions of a special natures illustrate the emphasis on increasing school enrollments. (Law 139, 1981).

11. Program for teaching and training, together with unifying the source of teacher education.

Law 139 of 1981 recognized the lack of university trained primary teachers and empowered the 5-year teacher training institutes to prepare teachers for the first grades of basic education. Teacher training for Basic Education has begun along with an assessment of teacher training institutes.

12. Buildings, equipment, and educational aids program.

The aim is to supply the appropriate number and type of educational buildings and equipment for various types and stages of education.

13. Educational administration.

The aim of this program is to develop the educational administration bodies, both central and non-central, with a view to increasing the efficiency of administrative and educational work.

14. Communication and data systems.

The objectives of this proposed system lie in getting up a network communication channels between center of performance and execution of education services on the one hand and the ministry on the other.

A project in communication and data collection was begun in 1982 but not completed until 1984. Fifteen people are to be trained in computers and data analysis in the United States. L.E.10,000 of a retention study went into the production of magnetic tapes. (Khalil, Y., personal interview, May 1983).

15. Educational research and innovation systems.

The general aim of this program is the development of the educational research and innovation staffs and processes in accordance with the demands of the comprehensive development plan.

16. Funding education.

The ultimate aim of this program is to supply the financial resources needed for the various aspects of education.

Internal budget allocations are made according to the expansion needs of the system. When increase percentage of students is expected or desired in a particular area, the cost for educating a student is multiplied by the projected enrollment to determine the financial allocation. No significant change in allocation has occurred in this process. (Khalil, Y., personal interview, May 1983).

17. Up-grading the competencies of primary school teachers.

The competencies of primary schools teachers in Cairo were assessed in 1980-81 by three professors of education--including the author. Ten graduate students from Ain Shams University used a nine-area observation instrument to observe and evaluate primary school teachers in nine educational zones of Cairo. (Mofti, Cochran, 1981, pp. 1-5). The Canadian International Development and Research Center provided $200,000 for extension of the research beyond Cairo. Primary school teachers throughout Egypt were surveyed on economic, social, and educational backgrounds in 60 different categories. (Report of Primary School Teachers, 1983,pp. 1-258). University training was begun for 5,000 primary school teachers at Ain Shams University in 1983-84. (Salama, A., personal interview, 1983).

The reorganization plan took existing programs and sharpened the educational goals. The difficulty in obtaining summative data on these projects resulted from the formative nature of data collection in the Ministry of Education. Only ministry officials in centralized administrative posts had documentation of results of projects thus far. The dissemination of this information was a laborious process executed by already overworked

officials.   Many of the concerns such as increasing
enrollment and improving the quality of primary and
secondary education had been long-term educational
goals.   What was apparent was that educational
programs without the legislative support of Law 139
did not make significant accomplishments.   But in
all of those areas reinforced by legislation,
significant accomplishments were made despite the
lack of financial resources.

CHAPTER VI REFERENCES

Canadian International Development and Research Center. (1982). "Statistics of Primary School Teachers," Government Printing, Cairo, ARE.

Cochran, J., Gaffar, A., Ebied, W., Mofti, M. (1981). "Training Assessment for Elementary Teachers in Greater Cairo," Journal of Education, Ain Shans University Press.

Ministry of Education. (1980). Comprehensive School Report, Cairo, ARE.

Ministry of Education. (1980). "Developing and Innovating Education in Egypt -- Policy, Plans, and Implementation Programs," National Center for Educational Research Publication, Cairo, ARE.

Ministry of Education. (1981). Experimental English Language Schools, Cairo, ARE.

Ministry of Education. (1979). "Working Paper on Development and Innovation of Education." Government Press, Cairo, ARE.

Ministry of Education, General Department of Statistics. (1980-81). "School Building Statistics," Cairo, ARE.

Reed, Stanley. (1981-82). "Dateline Cairo: Shaken Pillar," Foreign Policy, p.45.

Springborg, Robert. (1981, Winter, Vol. 24, No. 4). "U.S. Policy Toward Egypt: Problems and Prospects," Orbis.

World Bank and National Center for Educational Research. (1981). "First Level and Non-formal Education in the Arab Republic of Egypt," Government Press, Cairo, ARE.

Yacoub, Newal Kamal. (1982). "An Education of the Teaching of English in the Pre-Primary Stage in Experimental Language Schools." Unpublished master's thesis, Ain Shams University.

CHAPTER VII

FOREIGN INVESTMENT: U.S. AND WORLD BANK

        Sadat's Open Door Policy encouraged investment
in secular education from external sources. Foreign
assistance, mainly from USAID and World Bank, has
resulted in the allocation of millions of dollars to
education in Egypt. The proposals and plans
documented here are available in Egypt at the USAID
library, accessible to Americans and English-
speaking Egyptians who know of the library's
existence. Wherever summary or evaluation reports
were found, they were included. Of the 16 USAID
projectsproposed between 1974 and 1980, summary
documentation exists on the completions of only two
projects, the loan of one law professor to Cairo
University for two years and the textbook materials
project, both of which are described in the funded
proposals discussed below.
        The influx of Western and specifically American
aid from 1974 to 1980 did not make any significant
or even noticeable educational improvements in
Egypt. Political concerns prevented the effectiveness of the approximately $400 million USAID
allocation for education during this period. In
order to avoid another Iran where American presence
had been visible, USAID maintained a low profile,
further obscuring the evidence of the few completed
projects. And as Egypt was considered in the
developmental assistance category of U.S. government
assistance, each grant had to meet both Egyptian and
American governmental requirements. The first major
American effort in 1974, was the joint Egyptian-U.S.
Working Group on Education and Culture, which
focused on educational exchange, review of textbook
materials and the training of Egyptian teachers of
English. The following points were agreed upon by a
committee of high ranking American and Egyptian

governmental officials.

1. The U.S. was to invite qualified Egyptian leaders to the U.S. in each of the following areas: curriculum development, techniques of evaluation (especially examinations), concepts of technical education, and general co-operation between Egyptian and American universities.

2. The U.S. was to consult with UNESCO regarding a center for teacher education.

3. The U.S. was to assist the English Language Training Program at Ain Shams University.

*4. There was to be a study of each country's primary and secondary schooling, involving a review of textbook materials. A limited number of primary and secondary school teachers might also be exchanged.

5. The U.S. was to invite three Egyptian professors to lecture at American colleges.

6. Post-doctoral research grants were to go to two outstanding Egyptian senior scholars.

7. A special grant in archive management and museum was to be offered.

8. 3 American professors were to teach at Egyptian universities.

*9. 2 American professors were to come to Egypt to the International Law Center to lecture on international economic law.

10. Ten members of the Egyptian parliament were to visit the U.S. in 1975.

11. The U.S. was to offer grants to four or five Egyptians to study at recently established American cultural centers--in the fields of management, programming, skills related to community service, etc.

12. The U.S. was to provide experts in American drama.

13. Additional exchanges in technical education

93

and educational equipment were projected.
(Working Papers, 1976, pp. 14-15).

*Documentated as completed projects.

The Egyptian-U.S. Working Group on Education
and Culture project recommended that efforts of the
university community of Egypt be directed towards
developing sister-to-sister institutional relationships with U.S. universities of higher learning
which would result in a mutually beneficial
association. A plan was devised by representatives
of the joint working committees and the Egyptian
Bureau of Culture and Education to determine the
feasibility of establishing a program for Ain Shams
University and Alexandria University to visit Egypt
to determine areas of possible co-operation. The
conclusion of the initial visit (May 1975)
subsequently resulted in a pre-proposed grant to EPI
which included Cairo Ain Shams and Alexandria
universities. The grant award was for the purpose of
further exploring the feasibility of establishing a
co-operative assistance program compatible with
national needs, which would insure relevant
educational experiences capable of producing the
requisite manpower and research capability to
support the national plan for economic, social and
environmental development.

In an effort to develop a more viable program,
and separate from the terms of this grant, 12 short-
term consultants covering the physical and life
sciences and engineering were recruited by EPI from
its consortium and placed on assignment in Egypt
from October 10 through December 31, 1975. These
consultants, retained at the suggestion of the
Egyptian government, were financially supported by
the American government and the EPI consortium
universities.

The specific areas of concentrated assistance
were science, engineering, agriculture and medicine.
It was recognized that although specific assistance
was being requested for the separate disciplines,
each program would require a multi-disciplinary
approach addressing the economical, social and
cultural implications inherent in the introduction
of new technologies. These would be implemented in a
manner relevant to the needs of Egyptian society and
not devoted solely to academic and scholarly
achievements, as is all too common in some countries
where such assistance is being provided or is

contemplated.

    A. Ain Shams University would seek to strengthen its faculties of science and engineering to serve industry and government.

    B. Alexandria University would concentrate on developing a first-class national science research center--with some development in engineering--to serve the regional industry which comprises 30 percent of the total industry in Egypt.

    C. Cairo University would strive for excellence in establishing an institute for agriculture, with some development in medicine and the physical and life sciences.

It was further agreed that the character of the program of co-operative assistance would be designed to include the following components:

    A. Visiting Consultants -- short- and long-term.
    The primary responsibilities of the U.S. visiting consultants will be to assist the Egyptian faculties in:

        a. Up-grading and-or developing curricula

        b. Conducting joint research programs under joint supervision

        c. Identifying needed laboratory equipment and library materials in support of curricula and research

        d. Participating in the selection process for graduate fellowships abroad and local, that is, for study both in the U.S. and Egypt

        e. Teaching or offering faculty seminars (maximum of six credit hours) either in the faculty members major professional area or in new teaching methodologies such as self-paced learning, use of audio-visual aids, etc.

        f. Faculty exchange

The short-term exchange of Egyptian and U.S. professor-rank personnel for the purpose of offering lectures where appropriate and co-ordinating ongoing research programs.

g. Fellowships abroad
The selection of qualified Egyptian junior faculty for advanced degree training (Ph.D) in the U.S. and the provision of opportunities for both junior and senior faculty to participate in short-term refresher courses and in furthering joint research programs.

h. Fellowships locally
The granting of leaves of absence for qualified faculty to pursue advanced degree, training and-or relevant research at Egyptian institutions.

i. Equipment and library materials
The equipment and library materials deemed necessary to support curricula and research would be selected jointly and acquired locally where possible using Egyptian currency. The balance to be procured in the U.S. and shipped to Egypt.

j. EPI administrative support.

The total management of the program was be the responsibility of the permanent EPI staff. This would include financial and programmatic reporting, procurement, and all the program needs. An EPI field office was to be established or a subcontractual arrangement made with an existing organization. (The total investment in this component was to be $9,849,262.).

14. In 1978, a project proposal for improving the efficiency and relevancy of primary and secondary education and requiring approximately $200,000 was requested from AID ($80,654 + $132,000). Four major types of pilot programs were envisioned:

A. Programs which would change the style of lecturing from those consisting of

96

lecture-assign -- study-recite to those emphasizing learning to think-solve problems-apply to real-life situations. These programs also aimed to change teaching styles from one that used those textbooks only to those that used wide range of sources.

B. Program which would draw upon available resources of community to improve schools and vice versa (i.e. community schools).

C. Rescheduling of the schools year to get maximum use of facilities (all-year schools).

D. Comprehensive schools encompassing both general and technical programs. Schools were selected by a leadership task force proposed in the projects. (Mehain, 1978, pp. 1-15).

15. By 1980, the textbook portion of the 1974 decisions had expanded into a $36,000,000 project. An additional $2,500,000 was to go to the Central Agency for Books. The goals included:

A. The study and improvement of programs already running, including donation of textboks to university faculties in medicine, science, math, engineering, technology, and agriculture.

B. Long-range publishing in the form of USAID subsidy support for selling prices for American textbooks.

C. To provide educational and reference materials beyond the university level, to bring professionals up to date in public health, family planning, community development, agriculture, and technical-vocational education. Bibliography preparation to be the first focus.

D. Special surveys.

E. The project might add the training of

librarians and development of modern
library facilities. (Molenda, M., 1976).

Summary documentation of the completion of this
project reported that a permanent textbook display
was placed in the American Center in Cairo in 1977
and U.S. publishers participated at the Cairo
International Book Fair. The expenditure was
$350,000 for ordering and delivering 14,000 copies
of 3,000 U.S. titles which were then donated to the
university.(Childs, W., 1978, p. 1). The evaluation
report stated the needs of the students had not been
considered when ordering the textbooks. Adequate
bibliographic information did not exist. Moreover,
American publishers held back more current books in
order to sell off the older titles and the
attendants at the fair were unfamiliar with the
books. (Childs, p.3, 1978).

The projection of exchanges in technical
education had been modified as a vocational training
center in Cairo for skilled bus and truck
maintenance workers costing a total of $682,115
(with USAID support of $195,000). (Syndicate for
Land Transport,p.10). Although no summary report
was available in the USAID library in Cairo personal
interviews with four of the U.S. consultants working
on the project indicate that 30 bus mechanics were
enrolled in Heliopolis in 1984. The final report,
available in the USAID library in Washington D. C.
in 1985, stated the following; "One of the basis for
criticizing the curricula was that the vocabulary
level was for a literate population when 50-65% of
the target population are estimated to be
illiterate. Furthermore, the curricula was not
performance based, was written without the involvement of the target population and it was off-the-
shelf material." Since the curricula writers and
translator were Americans, paid handsome salaries by
any standard, it appeared that this project served
as employment for American professional and Egyptian
managers but did not necessarily meet Egyptian
training needs. Foreign (American) consultants,
publishers and equipment manufacturers benefited
from this project with little or no impact on the
mass educational system. . .especially when the
project was not open after three years of funding.

16. In 1979 another Joint Egyptian and American
team made plans to develop elementary
education (Basic Education). The goals of
the program were to:

A. Increase enrollment and spread educational opportunities equitably across Egypt.

B. Adapt education to regional needs.

C. Respond to growing needs for skilled workers and technicians.

D. To make young people be"responsible" citizens in Egypt.

General program areas suggested in this agreement included:

A. Piloting school building designs and construction for basic education schools, with attention to local design criteria, local participation, and local materials.

B. Development of a number of prototype pilot Basic Education instructional models, one or more for each governorate with particular attention to teacher utilization and effectiveness.

C. Strengthening of instructional materials, productions and distribution capacities, financial management, budget planning.

D. Development of a new education assessment-measurement system, and development and testing of procedures and instruments to facilitate this.

E. Expansion of planning, management training, and internal organization to become tasks of central MOE, as part of decentralization efforts.

F. Expansion and diversification of technical education options for students completing Basic Education.

G. Co-ordination of Basic Education schooling alternatives with non-formal skills training and adult education

99

opportunities. (Basic Education, 1979, p. 10).

In a memorandum dated March 4, 1980, Bernard Wilder wrote about the Basic Education in Egypt Survey stating, "During the first half of 1979 a contract team compiled a report for USAID/Cairo which provided an overview of basic education in Egypt and analyzed the weaknesses and potential of the educational system at this level. The report was accepted by both the Mission and the Egyptian Government and was given distribution in Egypt and in AID/W." This report, costing an estimated $300,000, was delivered to the Ministry of Education but never disseminated to ministry officials. (John Hofftenrichter, U. S. AID consultant, Gammal Nowier, National Center for Educational Research, 1983). The report was written by a Washington grant writer who never participated in the project and an American cultural anthropologist who was hired at the end of the project. (Andrea Rhue, Basic Education consultants, Byron Massialias, Basic Education consultant). The nature of the data contained in the report and the questionability of its accuracy made the report suspect to Egyptian officials. And yet, the U.S. government officials in Washington considered the project completed.

The 17 projects proposed from 1977 to 1980 by USAID did not mesh with the educational priorities established in the reorganizational plans for primary and secondary education or legislation enacted in 1981. Each of the projects was supposedly decided by a joint committee of American and Egyptian government officials and yet the projects funded were scattered in emphasis and not closely related to Ministry of Education or Supreme Council of Universities' goals. From 1976 to 1980, feasibility studies and programs were funded for training bus mechanics, textbook development, improving primary and secondary educational curriculum, and conducting all-year-round schools. Visible results from any of these programs funded between 1974 and 1980 are not easily found nor are there any evaluation reports readily available in Egypt. The USAID proposals then, served the function of obtaining money but not necessarily as a basis for execution. Interestingly enough, many of the feasibility studies were conducted by the same Americans--William Childs and Group 7. The exception seems to be the Basic Education Report which was neither recognized nor disseminated by the Ministry of Education. (USAID officer, Basic Education Report Consultants, personal interviews, 1982-83). Furthermore, when physical evidence of expenditure for proposed projects is sought, that, too, is difficult to find. For example, there is no evidence of the multi-media educational center developed by a 1982 Fulbright scholar. But, as he has never returned to Egypt, neither he nor the Washington officials who read his report realized that the fond memory of the students was all that remained of his 10 month "exchange."

Granted, it is difficult to locate reports which frequently disappear in a country that has an acute shortage of books. But the vocational training of some 30 bus mechanics in Heliopolis, a suburb of Cairo, would hardly be a highly visible project even though $37 million was to be spent on the project through 1983. However, bus mechanics do not form a central concern of the educational system. Furthermore, summary documentation is not available in Washington, D.C. in 1985 on the $2 million USAID in English language teacher training at Ain Shams with even though the U.S. withdrew participation in 1983. After the proposed allocation of millions of dollars, more significant results could be expected to be visible to both Americans and Egyptians. The major investment seemed to be the undocumented arrival and financing of teams of experts from America followed by the departures and financing of teams of Egyptian experts to the U.S. and the funding of myriads of joint American-Egyptian educational committees. Such tours and committees must have had an individual or perhaps potential importance, but the single description of the exchange of one law professor seemed to be neither significant nor valuable.

> Professor X arrived in Cairo in September 1978 under a host country contract with Cairo University. Almost immediately a conflict developed between those members of the law faculty who supported the activity and those who opposed it. Because of this conflict, the teaching role during the first year was minimal. He was only allowed to teach non-credit courses. In the two-year period, he ordered books, and designed one seminar on international contracts and one on international

arbitration. Two principal problems existed, both of which provide lessons for the future. First, the problem of lukewarm support form the law faculty stemmed in part from the Mission's reliance on a single person, the then dean of the law faculty. When that person departed, it became clear that most of the law faculty (generally French-oriented) had not been consulted and, indeed, may have feared an American legal invasion. Thus, the opposition which Professor X faced in his first year seems at least understandable. The second problem was the inordinate amount of time (both Professor X's and USAID Mission staff time) devoted to managing and monitoring the host country contract. Indeed, the contract should be Exhibit A to any brief advocating direct contracts for individuals, particulary where the host government organization is inexperienced in international contracting and has no need to develop a continuing expertise. The many problems involved with the furnishing of Professor X's flat and customs duties on his household effects largely fill two thick files on the modest activity. Finally, the host country nature (salary) of the contract exposed both Cairo University and Professor X to public criticism as to the contract amount. That is, the university had to identify with the compensation figures which, of course, included funds for commodities and short-term consultants as well as Professor X's salary and benefits.

The impact upon Egyptian education of USAID funding was not significant in view of the accomplishments--3,000 books which disappeared, an unsuccessful Book Fair, the training of 30 bus mechanics. Each of these completed projects reflects the political basis of USAID funding to Egypt which requires meeting both Egyptian and American governmental guidelines. While political agreements have been necessary it is questionable if politics should receive priority over achievements in an educational crisis which threatens the economic and social stability of the country.

In the early 1980's, the USAID leadership changed, and with that change, the proposals became more integrated with the Egyptian educational goals and some accomplishments began to emerge. Those proposals which meshed with the Ministry of Education goals received greater support. For example, a priority of increasing enrollment parallelled the U.S. proposal for construction of buildings for Basic Education. However, once again, political constraints prevented implementation of these projects. Basic Education buildings must be constructed with skilled Egyptian workers who do not exist in rural areas which meet the "low profile" American political requirement. Furthermore, negotiations regarding the manner of evaluating Basic Education material dissemination has not been completed despite months of joint U.S.-Egyptian negotiation. Those USAID proposals concerned with developing the infrastructure of the educational system such as developing curriculum materials and innovative teaching strategies were not implemented. And since each expenditure must have the approval of an Egyptian governmental official, the governmental or personal priorities of the men in power determined the proportion of expenditure. The result was that money was allocated but exact expenditure was determined by the political constraint of both American USAID and Egyptian administrators. Needs of the students and teachers, and implementation proposals were less important to the funding process.

By 1980, several five-year plans were made for over $250 million to be spent on Egyptian education. Major allocations were $10 million for for Basic Education facilities, $56 million for graduate education of Peace Fellowships for master's and Ph.D candidates and $26 million in University Linkages between American and Egyptian universities in areas of Egyptian developmental needs. In addition, there were individual grants to universities through such agencies as the Fulbright Commission, AmidEast, Catholic Relief Society, and the American Research Association, for research projects and technical and nutritional aid to schools. Egypt became one of the primary beneficiaries of U.S. development aid programs because of the Camp David Accords, making her the single largest aid recipient in the world.

And Egypt has been second only to Israel as a recipient of total U.S. foreign aid, which includes both economic and military assistance. According to a report issued by the American Embassy in Cairo, the U.S. invested over $51.5 million in joint research in Egypt through March 1981. (Katz, 1983, p. 2). Compared to the total $1 billion yearly U.S. expenditure in aid to Egypt, the $250 million allocation for education was small. (USAID official, personal interview, April 1983). However, expectations of Egyptian and American participants provides a profile of the process the U.S. followed in foreign aid to education.

The USAID expectation for each expenditure was based upon contracts whose provisions were mutually defined by Egyptian and American participants. The University Linkages allocation, for example, had to be a proposal instigated by an Egyptian university in an area of developmental need. The assumption was that the Egyptian institution not only knew its greatest areas of need but would also be able to identify appropriate people to initiate, organize and implementthe projects with co-operating U.S. universities. The financial allotment was restricted by the fact that grants categorized as developmental assistance had to be in developmental need areas designated by the Egyptian government.

Foreign aid is categorized in one of three ways; military assistance, multilateral aid (such as international banks like the World Bank), and bilateral assistance made between the U.S. and the government of the other country. USAID to education in Egypt is bilateral assistance and, as such, political in nature. The political complexity of implementing projects from USAID perspective is overwhelming. Due to Egyptian emigration to other countries, lack of necessary expertise, and lack of educated staffing, the Egyptian government cannot be expected to provide staffing assistance. Projects must follow the intent of U.S. Congress, the laws of Egypt and international agreements, all within the tensions and sensitivities existing in a politically strategic country. The administration of political USAID grants requires grant writing, documentation, project development, and monitoring for adherence to U.S. laws and regulations for 650 projects expending $1 billion yearly. If the director's office, management office, legal division, planning and comptroller's offices are deleted, the 125 USAID officials available to monitor projects numbers between 60 and 70 persons. The education division of

USAID suffers from the same general lack of
infrastructure. The result has been descriptions of
AID projects which parallel the descriptions of
Egyptian education projects as being slow in
implementation, overstudied as potential projects
and saturated with American contractors who do not
provide expertise if it is not available locally. In
addition, the "scattergram" approach to projects
appears to be poorly integratedand co-ordinated,
demonstrating a lack of knowledge of the Egyptian
educational system and a lack of long-range
planning.

For example, the $10 million allocated to
building facilities or renovating of existing
elementary and secondary schools is targeted for
geographic areas with no nearby schools or to high
density urban areas. "The expectation on the
American part was that the expenditure would in no
way significantly affect facility deficits but
rather was a small contribution to a major need. It
is hoped that building facilities within reasonable
walking distance from villages will increase the
female enrollment in schools which has been
disproportionately low." However, this is considered
"low absorption" of money as there are not enough
skilled workers in the country to construct
buildings even when money is allocated. (USAID
offical, personal interview, April 1983).

The largest appropriation of money is for
graduate training of Egyptians in U.S. institutions.
One program, called Peace Fellowships, has $57
million allocated. The candidate must first enroll
in an Egyptian University and then return to
graduate from the same institution. One of the pre-
requisites is the ability to understand English
which involves expenditures on English language
instruction. In 1981, 30 English teachers selected
by the Ministry of Education were sent to the U.S.
for a summer of training. The assumption is that
government school English language teachers will
train more proficient English language speakers.
These instructors were proceeded by 996 other
Egyptians trained in English language instruction
between 1975 and 1979 and another 850 in 1980.
(USAID document, 1980, p. 3). In addition, 500
potential Peace Fellow have been enrolled in English
Language Program at the American University in
Cairo. Tuition for all has been paid by American
aid. In 1984, 14 foreign faculty members were hired
to implement English Language Centers in rural
universities. (Bowers, personal interview, March,

1984). The predecessor of this program existed in the Princeton in Asia program begun in 1980. Recent American college graduates were placed in rural areas with a maximum of one week training in teaching English and two weeks training in Arabic. After two years of implementation, from 1980-1982, the program was abandoned as instructional materials and student atendance and progress were negligible. In the spring of 1982, the volunteers were brought back to Cairo and the programs were terminated. (Costa, M., Crump, P., personal interview, December 1982). The current plan is to replicate this Princeton in Asia failure with higher paid and better educated American instructors.

Another English language training investment was made from 1976 to 1985 at Ain Shams University. Called CEDELT, the Center for Educational Development of English Language Training, the project had ambitious goals. U.S. trained doctorate and master's personnel were hired to "interphase" with British and Egyptian counterparts in developing materials and training Egyptian teachers of English. The project continues to be funded by the British Council but the Americans withdrew in 1982, having spent $2,000,000 and having obtained negligible support from the Egyptian government. (CEDELT director, personal interview, 1982). The British continue to work on the development of material and host visiting USAID-sponsored consultants.

Emphasis on the English proficiency for graduate training has meant the selection of candidates for Peace Fellowships are made from elite Egyptians who already speak English; thus, persons not central to areas of developmental needs may be selected. For example, one can travel to Tanta, an industrial and agricultural city of 2 million and find only limited English spoken, thus restricting the opportunity people in rural areas from obtaining Peace Fellowships. And yet English proficiency is critical. Arabic and French are the languages most commonly spoken by younger Egyptians as Nasser discouraged the teaching of English and Peace Fellowships are not given to those over 35.

The rationale for the Basic Education, University Linkages, and Peace Fellowship programs seems to be interaction with the Egyptian educational system without dictation of control. Financing of graduate study, construction of facilities in low visibility areas, and obtaining U.S. institutional expertise from universities fill a vacuum that would not be filled without U.S.

support. The Egyptians decide on their areas of need, then the American representatives conduct needs assessments, set selection procedures and identify monitoring agents. In this way, the control of the project remains in the hands of the Egyptians. (USAID official, personal interview, April 1983).

Unfortunately, many Egyptians do not realize the degree of control that they have over the projects conducted in their country. Al Ahram Al Iktisidi, a major Egyptian political and economical magazine, published a series of articles "exposing" American "infiltration" in Egypt. (October and November 1982). In these articles, a variety of critics, the majority academics, commented on American involvement in research which is perceived as a serious threat to Egypt's territorial and cultural integrity.

Research projects illustrate the manner in which Americans retain the right to influence if not decide how their financial resources are spread out over various developmental projects in Egypt. Each research project which is "jointly funded" includes at least one American researcher co-operating with an Egyptian professor and a number of Egyptian data collectors. Often Egyptian and American researchers are paid on different salary scales, as reported in the law professor exchange. This further limits the co-operation between Egyptian and American researchers. It is difficult for an Egyptian researcher who may have earned his doctorate in England or the U.S. to perceive how his or her skills could be less valuable just because he or she happens to be Egyptian. However tolerant the financing agency is with the researcher, it necessarily restricts him or her by the selection of the topic, the points on which the researcher should focus and in many cases the way of handling them. (Al Ahram Al Iktisidi, p.8). University Linkages are a case in point, as they must address an area of developmental need and must be initiated by an Egyptian university. Delegations from American universities with ready-made proposals arrive in Egypt. Satisfying USAID standards is difficult for native-speaking Americans, much less for officials at Egyptian Universities, which are understaffed and have limited English typing facilities. The result is that some American universities design and write the projects, allocating themselves substantial control of the project if they desire.

Egyptians have been especially sensitive to the

AID developmental assistance funding with "strings" attached, since Israel receives a monthly AID check categorized as direct assistance which it can use at its own discretion without the accompaning AID bureaucracy. The U.S. could give Egypt cash, as it does Israel, but fears corruption. (Reed, 1981, p. 178). Furthermore, the dangerous point is not so much related to the process of collecting data in itself as it is to allowing the Americans to use the data in a way which might be contrary to the good of the country. (Al Ahram El Iktisidi, October 18, 1982, p.8). In fact, Egyptians have little or no control over how the information is obtained in Egypt itself. This could be due to inadequate libraries or translation abilities of the universities. It must be pointed out that Egyptian data gathering, and information storage and retrieval capabilities are such that information gathered in these research projects could not be expected to reach personnel who need it rapidly. But the Balkanization of university research (and the proprietary attitude toward information exchange) restricts knowledge of and exchange of research. There can be little institutional co-operation at the level of research practitioners. USAID funding, partly because it finances overly restricted and focused research projects, and partly because it puts money into the existing system, contributes to the competition between universities. For example, Ain Shams was the location of the CEDELT project, not Cairo University. Therefore, any project material developed at Ain Shams was not easily utilized at Cairo University.

Whether or not the information gathered through research is available in Egypt, the lack of centralization and communication regarding research findings and their use constitutes a vulnerability to the country. The topics discussed in Al Ahram Al Iktisidi were so sensitive that eight pages were deleted before it was published. In a country in which newspapers, books, television and films are censored this open investigation definitely constitutes a threat to the status quo.

On the other hand, examples of unrestricted American technical aid in higher education have been funded in the Fulbright Senior Lectureships. Reinstated in 1978, the lectureships have increased in number and cost each year. Each senior Fulbright is selected by the U.S. President's Board of Foreign Scholars and the participating country. In Egypt, U.S. funds pay for transportation of the grantees and their spouses, education for their children and their salary comparable to what they would earn in the States. This includes reduced-cost housing at approximately $220 a month, and $600 to be spent on books. In 1982-83, the Egyptian universities were asked to share in the cost of the grantees by paying part of the stipend. But by even paying just a portion of the salary, Egyptian universities are paying more than twice the base salary of an Egyptian full professor. The locations of the assignment and selection of grantee specialization are established by the Binational Fulbright Commission, while responsibilities and assignments are decided by the host institution. Because the Egyptian institution determines the specialization desired, the actual assignment to be completed, and the manner in which it is carried out, the Fulbright program qualifies as unrestricted aid of the kind desired by Egyptians.

Assessments of the value of their technical assistance documented in Fulbright reports have been mixed. Generally, the experience depends upon the university and the Egyptian colleagues. Field researchers and those who were given large assignments, even as much as 26 course hours, felt the experience benefited both themselves and Egypt. (Brunag, personal interview,1981). However, in the departments in which the majority of the professors resided elsewhere, the Fulbright Scholars regretted the limits on professional exchange. Other professors taught only one class, found their expertise under-utilized, and searched for activities to make themselves useful. (Kranston, 1979, Kramer, 1980, Benton, 1983, Newell, 1983).

Even a reasonable assignment cannot necessarily be accomplished in a 10-month residence. American professors with limited prior experience abroad must learn to operate in educational processes which are unfamiliar, such as evaluation differences and unexpected class schedule changes. "Physical conditions are so bad that, quite frankly, I dreaded going out to the university and felt all the symptoms of incipient panic whenever I was there. Conditions were more than uncomfortable; they were positively threatening." (King, Fulbright report 1981). Thus, the provision of technical assistance requires a longer period for the grantee to become effective. In fact, students from undergraduate to beginning graduate levels have complained to senior lecturers about the lack of continuity in experience, even with 10-month grantees. By the time

students get used to the Americans and appreciate
them, they are gone. Egyptian colleagues, including
department chairpersons, have expressed the same
sentiments. From the American perspective, the more
people who come to Egypt and experience the
exchange, the more egalitarian the program seems. In
other countries where Fulbright Scholars have been
institutionalized, universities are accustomed to
having a Fulbright professor teach certain courses.
What is not recognized is that Americans are used to
institutional continuity. They don't realize that
institutional bases aren't as prominent in Egypt and
that, in fact, the culture argues against it. For
example, there is no Egyptian institutional record
of Fulbright contributions other than the book
purchases at any university once the grantees have
departed. The reports which grantees are required to
write are sent out to government officials in the
States, but there is no mechanism for sending them
to Egyptian officials. Therefore, the significance
of the assignment is basically built on the personal
relationships that are established. If language
barriers or social isolation or marginal assignments
prevent these relationships from being formed, the
instructional contribution is difficult to measure.
This is especially true because exams and grades are
a collective faculty effort, and thus grantees may
not compose or grade their students' final work, or
assign grades given after their departure. The
preference of the Binational Fulbright Commission,
and, as far as can be determined, of the Egyptian
educational establishment for relatively short-term
Fulbright lectureship assignments, works against the
development of technical assistance continuity in
this relatively successful example of unrestricted
American aid.

While results are difficult to verify, the
exact expenditure in each of the USAID projects is
even more difficult to determine. It is certain
that the U.S. policy has been to keep a low profile.
This policy, compounded by lack of USAID officials
to staff and monitor programs, may have contributed
to the lack of visible results from USAID
expenditures. Also, there are individual Egyptian-
American institutional connections which are not
categorized under USAID aid to education such as the
Massachusetts Institute of Technology project at
Cairo University and National Science Foundation
projects which increase the amount of U.S. funding
but are not considered USAID education projects. In
1979, the USAID was the "foremost source of

assistance" for research grants as it approved 253
projects for various ministries and organizations to
be funded from PL480 (surplus wheat funds) to the
approximate amount of $44 million. The agreement of
the U.S. Agency for International Development
(USAID) includes seven projects for the Ministry of
Agriculture valued at $22.5 million. The U.S.
Scientific and Technological the Cooperation
agreement provides for the implementation of
research activities and projects by the Academy of
Scientific Research and Technology within a sum of
$8.1 million for the first stage. (Scientific
Research and Technology Group,p. 54). The projects
between 1977 and 1980 had the money allocated, but
summary documentation existed in the Cairo-based
USAID library on two projects which emerged from the
proposals--the Cairo Book Fair, and the exchange of
one law professor. The Book Fair was not succesful,
according to the evaluation report. The bus
mechanics project began training in 1983 but no
summary report was in the USAID library in Cairo.
RCA, the bus mechanics contractor, hired four
Americans' to write the bus mechanics curriculum,
which was completed without having been piloted on
Egyptian students and there was difficulty in
conducting an initial needs assessment. (Evaluation
Report Project 263-0114, p. 51). American English
language training with CEDELT completed the
development of training materials despite the lack
of students to be trained. The materials were
published in 1982 but unfortunately require people
knowledgable in the innovative approaches used in
them in order to utilize the material. (Sayers, B.,
Thornton, L., Strain, J., personal interview, 1982).
Of the two completed projects, neither had
educational significance or number of participants
as a criteria for execution. One USAID official
described all other projects as excuses for Egyptain
officials to go to the U.S. and U.S educators to
come to Egypt. But as documentation was not
available on the programmatic benefits of these
exchanges, verification is not easily made.
Personal interviews with American consultants
working on funded projects indicate general
dissatisfaction with the results and utilization of
their products. But the USAID allocations continue
to arrive, even though results are questionable.
Table 11 reveals USAID financial expenditure as of
March 1983.

TABLE 11

Project Title	Oblig.	Total Expend.	Unexpended Balance
HUMAN RESOURCES & DEVELOPMENT CO-OPERATION (HRDC)			
Office of Education & Training (EDU)			
Programs (Projects)			
Tec. Trans. & Manpower Dev.	34,500	22,082	12,418
Dev. Plann. Studies	15,795	11,475	4,320
Vocational Trg. for Product.	17,500	42	17,458
Peace Fellowships	54,000	14,352	39,648
Vehicle Maint. Trg.	4,500	2,437	2,063
University Linkages	27,500	1,729	25,771
Basic Education	39,000	4,079	34,921
Sub-Total HRDC/EDU	192,795	56,196	136,599
Office of Science & Technology (ST)			
Programs (Projects)			
Applied Science/Tech. Res.	24,400	9,507	14,893
Manag. Develop. for Product.	8,500	1,256	7,244
Indust. Tech. Applications	10,000	445	9,555
Mini.,Petro., & Gr. Assess.	20,700	1,113	19,587
Energy Policy & Renew.	7,800	-0-	7,800
Sub-Total HRDC/ST	71,400	12,321	59,079
Office of Health (H)			
Programs (Projects)			
Str. Rural Health Del. Ser.	7,800	5,369	2,431
Urban Low Cost Health	37,253	6,580	30,673
Suez Comm. Health Pers. Trg.	8,100	3,062	5,038
Diarrheal Diseases	26,000	227	25,773
Sub-Total HRDC/H	79,153	15,238	63,915
Office of Population (P)			
Programs (Projects)			
Family Planning	67,400	35,995	31,405
Sub-Total HRDC/P	67,400	35,995	31,405

The bulk of USAID expediture has been on exchange programs for Egyptian and American university students and faculty. The benefits of these exchanges are again difficult to measure on a national basis. The skills or knowledge acquired and its applicability to the Egyptian educational system cannot be determined. "The Peace Fellowship program is moving well toward the upwardly revised target of 1,900 graduate level participants in U.S. universities by the end of 1986. Intensive interviewing of returned Peace Fellows in Cairo and Alexandria indicates that Peace Fellows are of high caliber and in general are already making contributions to Egyptian development." This is true of those participants who return to research institutes or private sector positions. But those who return to Egyptian government ministries and agencies are frustrated and disappointed. "They are chagrined at such situations as unimaginative supervisors, skimpy operating budgets, lack of computers and other equipment, and the perceived long, undue wait to receive promotions and other benefits." It is evident to the Egyptian people that the U.S. is supplying aid to Egypt, some Egyptians are getting richer and going to the States and Americans are becoming more visible in Egypt. Foreigners spend money, but the educational benefit of their presence has not been apparent. The beneficiaries of capital inflow are small in number and are clustered at the urban-elite end of the socio-political continuum--a consequence, in part, of the structure of the Egyptian political economy.

Moreover, rampant corruption only further frustrates the effective use of incoming capital. Innumerable Egyptian professionals and bureaucrats have climbed aboard the USAID gravy train and are riding it for all they're worth, which, in an increasing number of cases, is quite a lot. Enjoying high disposable incomes, they of course are in search of purchases and pleasures, further discrediting themselves, their government, and American assistance in the process. (Springborg, 1981, p. 311).

> No doubt much of the blame for the writing of unproductive dry linkage agreements rests squarely on American academic entrepreneurs who gouge a round-trip excursion ticket out of their own university development

> office, visit Egypt during the mid-
> year break when the weather in Cairo
> beats that in Chicago, and have to
> have some document in hand, to prove
> the candle was worth the cost, when
> they return home. Some do stop by
> the AID-Cairo office just before
> dashing for the airport, believing in
> all innocence that such good works
> will be rewarded by a bundle of cash.
> In even greater innocence, some may
> be unaware that AID has an entire
> factory devoted to the generation of
> its own projects and hardly needs
> their journeyman labor. (Reed, 1981,
> p. 45).

Among the numerous AID activities in addition
to its participant training program is that for what
are called "Strengthening Grants" for American land
grant institutions. These derive from the Title XII
amendment to the International Development and Food
Assistance Act of 1975 and provide matching funds up
to $300,000 annually to strengthen capacities of
these institutions in teaching, research, extension
and advisory services in the fields of agriculture
(including fisheries), food, nutrition, and rural
development.

At present there are five of these with Egypt,
involving Auburn University, California State
University at Fresno, Colorado State University,
Iowa State University, and the University of
Nebraska, though in addition Montana State
University has signed a memorandum of understanding
with the agriculture faculty of Alexandria
University in anticipation of a "Strengthening
Grant."

While all have exchange potential and U.S.
funding, it does not follow that all of them tie in
with Egyptian universities' needs. That of Colorado
State relates to the Ministry of Irrigation as a
water use and management project, and is intended
during five years to provide short courses for 20
Egyptians, on-the-job training for 80 to 100, and
higher studies in the United States for four. Begun
in 1977 at a projected total cost of $1.86 million,
this project further illustrates how difficult it is
to peg such enterprises as university "linkages,"
for in truth Colorado State is but the lead
university for the Consortium for International
Development based in Tucson. In turn, Colorado

State views the work in Egypt as part of its larger
concern with "Arid and Semi-Arid Areas" embracing
Nigeria, Kenya, Brazil, Venezuela, Peru, and
Lesotho, and has had a long-standing project of
similar nature in Pakistan, also AID funded.
(Boewe, 1981, p. 89,90).

Such grants demonstrate why Egyptians find it
personally difficult to implement American programs
or to give credit to American funding and expertise.
Historically, foreigners have occupied the country
and have constructed educational projects for their
own occupational or nationalistic needs. For
example, Mohammed Ali did begin the first schools
for administrators, veterinarians, accountants,
doctors, and technicians. These schools did not
survive after his death in 1849 as his successors
were not as interested in military conflict and did
not need such schools. Lord Cromer, the British
agent general, constructed English language
instruction institutions which prepared Egyptians to
conduct the British occupational policies. During
these periods of occupation, the Egyptians were
educated in religious schools and the select,
wealthy Egyptians attended secular foreign schools.
With the surge of nationalism under Nasser, the
dichotomy between the rich, secular and foreign-
sponsored Egyptians and poor Egyptians was reduced.
Sadat re-instituted this dichotomy with the
encouragement of foreign investors, specifically
foreign developmental assistance in education. The
Egyptian educator then, who supports elite secular
educational projects of the foreigners finds
himself, as a result of history, aligned with the
foreign occupier. Egyptians are experiencing a
deterioration in the mass educational system and
foreigners become a target for their frustrations.
For example, one vocal anti-American English
language student was not even aware his tuition was
being paid by USAID. (Kassabgy, personal interview,
1983). Furthermore, when enormous amounts of money
are supposedly spent and there is no significant or
noticeable result, Egyptians have reason to suspect
foreign interests are receiving top priority.

If the opinions stated in Al Iktisidi were a
genuine reflection of the attitude toward Western
funding (and there is a question about this), the
acquisition is seen as yet another form of foreign
occupation. The memory of the British manipulation
of education for their own country's needs does not
seem that different from the American aid. American
organizations and universities and technicans

administer grants to meet their own needs and enhance their own individual and institutional finances. American money is sent to Egypt and spent on American companies, American consultants and select Egyptians. The presence of Americans increases and the conditions in primary, secondary and higher education deteriorate. And for some, American or western presence provided a convenient scapegoat for the problems of the country. But more than that, the statement for American generosity, expertise and support was not well made.

Not only America but also other countries and international groups such as UNESCO and World Bank are contributing to Egyptian educational development. The World Bank projects provide a different model of foreign investment. In order to acquire money, Egypt must belong to the International Monetary Fund organization and must qualify for International Development Association (IDA) money by having a per capita yearly average below $690. World Bank members representing 146 countries appoint governors who sit on the Board of Directors. This board approves loans once documentation has been made of development plans, and of appraisal team feasibiltity studies. The bank provides technical assistance and administration and monitoring units but Egyptians are assumed to have the capability, manpower and resources to evaluate their own programs. The bank has a mission which visits the country but the primary responsibility for implementation rests with the Egyptians.

The World Bank conducted three educational projects for Egypt beginning in 1976. The cost of the first project was estimated at $54.2 million with a foreign exchange component of $22.2 million. The money has been completely disbursed, accomplishing the following goals:

1. expand, diversify, improve training of technicians, skilled and semi-skilled workers;

2. introduce comprehensive preparatory and secondary schooling to provide more instruction in practical courses;

3. increase and upgrade training of technical teachers and workshop instructors;

   Components included:

a. construction, furniture, equipment and technical assistance for twenty building trades vocational centers, three building trades instructor training centers, two technical training institutes

b. furniture and-or equipment and technical assistance for one lower secondary and two upper secondary diversified pilot schools, four technical training schools, three technical training institutes, one technical teacher training school, ten industrial-vocational training centers, one industrial instructor training center

c. pre-investment engineering design and-or technical assistance for three lower secondary and two upper secondary diversified pilot schools, three primary teacher training colleges, six technical training schools, four technical training institutes, five industrial-vocational training centers;

d. technical assistance for educational planning studies.

The program projected an annual output of 17,000 semi-skilled and building trade workers, 64,000 technicians and instructors, and 2,300 skilled industrial workers. There were pre-investment designs of additional comprehensive lower and upper secondary schools, primary teacher training colleges, and vocational-technical training institutes, with a possible second World Bank project to improve formal education. The planned date of execution was July 1977. (World Bank Document, 1977).

The second educational project expanded the goals of the first project in technical training. The following goals stipulated expansion and improvement of educational manpower, research and planning, management training in the industry and construction sector, population education in public schools, and training opportunities for the urban poor.

Construction trades and handicraft components would cater exclusively to the urban poor, train approximately 7,200 skilled workers annually and

jointly comprise 30 percent ($25.5 million) of the
$58.8 million project costs using 20 percent of the
foreign currency required. The United Kingdom agreed
to provide technical assistance input of
approximately $1 million. The second project was to
begin January 26, 1977. As of 1983, $22.9 million
or over half the money had been disbursed.

The third project, scheduled to begin March 2,
1981, was preceded by 11 months of preparation.
The total grant was for $38 million and as of 1983
had not been disbursed. The goals included:

1. Expansion, diversification, and improvement
   of the training of technicians and skilled
   and semi-skilled workers in order to meet
   urgent manpower needs.

2. Assistance to and improvement of the quality
   of lower and upper secondary education
   through provision of diversified practical
   training to all students.

3. Increase and improvement of the training of
   primary, secondary, and technical teachers
   and instructors.

4. Improvement of educational and manpower
   research and planning.

5. Increase and improvement of management
   training in industry and construction
   sectors.

6. Expansion and improvement of population
   education in public schools to achieve these
   objectives, the capital and technical
   assistance provides for 25 new and 35
   existing vocational, agricultural and
   handicraft skills. Training centers and
   agricultural information centers were to add
   1,200 managers and 4,400 skilled and semi-
   skilled workers to the work-force, up-grade
   capabilities of 1,200 managers, 750
   extension personnel, and 750 skilled workers
   for agriculture; train 6,000 farmers and
   through an educational materials center
   reach approximately 40,000 farmers. A health
   science resources center was to improve
   services provided by rural and district
   health centers. 60 percent of the program's
   credit proceeds were aimed at low-income

groups.

The total cost of the third program was $56.9 million with $2.4 million to go to Assuit and Cairo universities for the implementation of related programs.

The first project ended December 31, 1980; and was considered "satisfactory." Virtually all technical assistance was completed. Approximately 90 percent of all equipment was procured and nearly all installed. Of the 23 institutions to be constructed, 17 were completed and operational, while five more were expected to be operational by October 1980, the other by December 1980. All the existing institutions which had been re-equipped were operational. By December 1980, approximately 80 percent of the credit amount was disbursed and all the remainder was committed.

The second project which began in 1979 and will finish in 1984 was considered proceeding "very well." Of the 23 institutions to be constructed, 10 were completed by 1981 and three Ministry of Higher Education Institutes were finished in 1983. All equipment was under procurement with contracts signed for approximately 50 percent of budget as of 1983. All technical assistance was contracted and implementation was nine months ahead of schedule.

In 1983, a third vocational technological training grant for approximately $38 million was signed by the World Bank in co-operation with the Ministry of Housing and the Ministry of Industry. While concerned with training, this grant is not related to the Ministry of Education and hence is outside the "educational" administrative category. All the proposals cited were of necessity modified in both expenditure and even location during the implementation process. Overall directions and approximate allocations are accurate with the emphasis upon technological training and supportive services.

A major difference between USAID and World Bank proposals is the classification of information and focus of projects. The World Bank proposals are readily available but documentation is classified. Although World Bank assistance has been primarily in vocational technical training, conducted independently of the formal educational system, it is interesting to note their projects integrate with both the developmental needs and goals of the society and the priorities of the reorganization plan. The World Bank has integrated development assistance into the educational and cultural needs of Egypt. The World Bank projects are evaluated by officials who come to the country for a short period and then write their report. This system does not increase the visibility of World Bank investors.

But the long-term effect of externally funded projects as described by El Koussy provide reason to suspect the "satisfactory" nature of any foreign investment.

> We can, therefore, state that any partial amelioration within the existing pattern will temporarily lead to an ostensible improvement, but will soon revert to the general run of things. It should be noted that numerous ameliorations were introduced in Egypt, but were all finished and done with by the hubbub of the existing system. Modern apparatuses were provided to be neglected and kept in storerooms, model schools were constructed only to fall back within the familiar school pattern, the laboratories were made available only to be closed and school libraries were provided, but not used by teacher or pupil, and school papers were introduced but never amounted to anything. There are, therefore, two essential factors on which we must agree. Firstly, we must think for the future of a radical change, dispensing with the present system, putting up with it only temporarily. Secondly is to formulate an overall comprehensive plan and give no thought to partial issues unless they are perfectly clear in the overall comprehensive plan. (El Koussy, 1977, p. 45).

The educational success of the projects, however, is not the primary concern of the World Bank. Their focus is that money is disbursed and the loan is repaid. The difficulty with examining developmental assistance is that USAID, World Bank, and Egypt have different criteria for determining success. In simplistic terms, the U.S. goal is political: to maintain economic and social stability in a pro-Western country. And since the signing of the Camp David Accords in 1979 and the concomitant influx of USAID, Egypt has not participated in a war. This peace agreement solidified Egypt's relationship with the U.S. but alienated other Arab countries. In March 1979, the Arab League voted to exclude Egypt from membership. The country, which had only recently been indentified with Arab unity under Nasser, had just so quickly lost its Arab identity when Sadat spoke for all "Arabs" and peace. In the political sense, USAID criteria for success have been met by the reluctance of Egypt thus far to participate in Middle Eastern conflicts.

Egypt's criteria for successful foreign investment differs from that of the World Bank and USAID. The existing educational system is one which emphasizes religion as the cultural basis of the country. This basis must be supported if new technology is to be assimilated or accommodated into the current educational system. Both USAID and World Bank funding have been structured so as to avoid influencing the cultural education of the Egyptian masses. The World Bank contributions have been administered by the Ministries of Housing and Industry and thus do not threaten the Ministry of Education. Furthermore, World Bank training differs from education in that it does not propose to teach values along with the procedures of training in such areas as welding, plumbing, and electrical wiring. USAID educational financing focused on the accommodation or assimilation of expenditures in programs which have a low visibility in society. The Peace Fellowship candidates and those targeted for English language training are selected by the Egyptian ministries. The Basic Education grant will spend the bulk of its money on buildings in regions where population density is not high, with $10 million being spent on instructional materials, such as maps, which do not interphase with the cultural basis. And finally, the University Linkages expenditures are administrative arrangements which may not be readily apparent to the average Egyptian and certainly not altering the cultural emphasis of the country as both Linkages and Peace Fellowships are concerned with university level students. The result is a concerted effort to assimilate into the existing educational system in areas which do not affect the cultural basis. However, the lack of visibility of the American expenditure in particular has led to suspicions of graft and confusion regarding the actual expenditure of the money when little benefit results. This confusion is also shared by the American public as they read in the _Wall Street Journal_ and elsewhere that the U.S. aid to Egypt is disappearing in bureaucratic mazes.

The failure of USAID to make a significant contribution to Egyptian education, despite increased expenditure, does not detract from the success of gaining peace in the Middle East which is a major tenet of U.S. political strategy. The cost of investing a few million dollars in education in Egypt with no return costs far less than the deployment of troops. (Educational Director, USAID, personal interview, 1983). The long range benefits of educating a society to address its domestic needs seems lost in this short-term militaristic perspective. However, the continued U.S. financial support in Egypt aids the economic base of the country and hence improves the World Bank's probability of repayment. Egyptians on the other hand, have an immediate need for expanding educational facilities and improving the capabilities of the graduates to address acute economic, social, and political problems. There is a need to alleviate imbalances and integrate a society divided by a history of religious education for the masses and secular education for the elite. Unfortunately USAID and World Bank investments have increased rather than reduced this division. The Egyptian criteria of successful educational projects differ significantly from that of USAID and World Bank. They want the equipment, facilities, and technical training but not necessarily the potential cultural impact from educational projects which alter the existing power and societal infrastructure.

Foreign aid to education, as it is currently constituted, poses a severe threat to the delicate imbalances in Egyptian society. The Egyptian ambition is to retain the economic aid from Western countries such as the U.S., Germany, Japan, and France and continue to maintain the Egyptian culture. Successful American educational aid projects, if completed, could further divide society--and perhaps increase secular power. The more money provided to westernized Egyptian administrators, politicians, and technologists, the greater the polarization becomes between the religious and secular factions in the country. It was this increasing gap which Sadat was unable to bridge.

Egypt's political alienation from other Arab countries as a result of the Camp David agreement

increased the activity of the Muslim Brotherhood. In
August and September of 1981, the government began
to arrest Islamic and Coptic fundamentalists. On
October 6, 1981, Sadat was assassinated by a group
of 22 men representatives of the Muslim Brotherhood.
The statement seemed to be one which reinforced the
return to religious and cultural values of the past
and against the foreign development and directorship
of the country. Vice-President Hosni Mubarak
succeeded Sadat as president and as a former general
in the army, he provided a continuity of military
leadership begun by Nasser and Sadat... men of the
people educated by the British when there was a need
for Egyptian military leadership. As of 1985,
Mubarak had begun a gradual reduction of foreign
imports and investments and the subtle closing of
Sadat's "open door" policy.

CHAPTER VII REFERENCES

A.I.D. document. (1980). "Development of Related English Language Training Needs and Resources," Cairo, A.R.E.

Al Ahram Al Iktsidi. (1982). "Report on American Research," October, November.

Boewe, Charles, (1981) American Egyptian Educational Exchange, Lexington, Kentucky.

Bowers, R. (1981). "Center for Developing English Language Teaching: Summary of Evaluation Report and Recommendations and Notes on Their States," CEDELT.

Childs, Willliam. (1978). "University Texbook Program Component of the University Instructional Material and Library Project, Final Report, Recommendations, and Observations," International Publishing Services, McLean, Virginia.

El Koussy, Abdel. (1977). "The Need for Change," The Specialized National Councils Magazine, Presidency of the Republic ARE, 4.

Evaluation Report for Project 263-0114, Government Document, pp. 8, 51.

Ibrahim, Saud. (1981). "Superpowers in the Arab World," Presentation of a joint CSIS-Al Ahram Conference, Proceedings, Vol. 4, #3.

Katz, Greg. (1983). "Education," Cairo Today, February.

McLain, J. D., Director. (1978). "Strategies for Implementation of Selected Pilot Programs to Improve Efficiency and Relevancy of Primary and Secondary Education in Egypt," JF00 EG-AAA-492.

Meeting of the Joint Egyptian-U.S. Working Group on Education and Culture. (1976). "Working Papers," available from USAID Library, Cairo, A.R.E.

Molenda, Michael. (1978). "University Instructional Material; Educational Technology Component," Concept paper, Bloomington, Indiana, February 6, Available from USAID Library, Cairo, A.R.E.

Reed, Stanley. (1981-82). "Dateline Cairo: Shaken Pillar," Foreign Policy, 45.

Report of the Joint Egyptian-American Team. (1979). "Basic Education in Egypt," JF20 EG-AAA-693.

Scientific Research and Technology Group. "Toward a Long-Term Scientific Research Plan," The Specialized National Councils Magazine, 9.

Springborg, Robert. (1981). "U.S. Policy Toward

Egypt: Problems and Perspectives," Orbis, 34, 4.

Syndicate for Land and Transport. "Study to Determine Feasibility of Establishing Vocational Training Centers in Cairo for Skilled Bus and Truck Mechanic Workers," JF50 EG-AAA-698.

CHAPTER VIII

GUIDELINE FOR FOREIGN DEVELOPMENTAL ASSISTANCE
1970 - 1983

If stability and economic and social
development are the desired products of foreign
investment, then the educational institution must be
given priority.   Lack of knowledge or interest in
the established educational organization and culture
results in financial expenditure without significant
and appreciated results. Involved personnel, for a
period of time, receive additional salary, and
machinery is purchased. But change on the part of
the personnel or utilization of equipment within the
existing system is not guaranteed. It is essential,
therefore, for foreign aid projects to be either
assimilated or accommodated within the existing
educational system.
Accommodation, meaning an addition to the
present system, occurs when a component of the
proposed program already exists. The university
textbook program at Cairo University and CEDELT at
Ain Shams University are two examples of externally
supported projects which supplemented and required
accommodation into already existing educational
components. As the goals of the materials project
state, the project's goal was to study and improve
existing programs, such as the donation of textbooks
to university faculties in medicine, science, math
and engineering, technology, and agriculture.
(Childs, 1978, p. 1). One of the projects prepared
an American exhibit at the Cairo International Book
Fair, an annual event which is not a component of
the formal educational system. The summary report of
the   success of that exhibit stated that needs of
the students had not been identified nor taken into
account when ordering the textbooks. Adequate
bibliographic information, which was another
component of the textbook project, had not been

conducted. Moreover, it was found that publishers met their own needs and held back more current books in order to sell off the older titles and attendants at the fair were not familiar with the books. (Childs, 1978, p. 2). Neither the established educational organization nor the culture were considered in this unsuccessful project. CEDELT project repeated the same mistakes and also had less than expected results. The initial intention was to offer a master's degree in English language teaching at Ain Shams University. But rather than build the project as an addition to the existing Egyptian English language program, the CEDELT project established a separate reference library and duplicating center, and teaching materials taught by predominately British or American staff. The result was that after five years of operation, students who had graduated from the center were required by the Egyptian Ministry of Education to take additional courses and write a mini-thesis if they wished to continue for a doctorate in a university or to be given credit for a master's within the Egyptian system. (CEDELT graduates, personal interviews) The material developed at Ain Shams was not even used at the university itself, but rather was piloted in other universities. (CEDELT American and British staff, personal interviews, 1980-1982) Furthermore, no students were sent by the Ministry of Education to take courses, as the program was not accommodated into the existing educational framework. The results of both the Book Project and CEDELT, representing U.S. expenditures of over $2.5 million, were not as significant as expected because they attempted to create new or parallel functions independent of ongoing Egyptian components.

One means of accommodating a foreign aid project into the existing system is to begin with recommendations and reports already compiled by earlier committees or needs-assessment teams. Reports describing development needs and interphasing of educational programs exist in archives, ministries, and research centers. The General Administration of Statistics has the responsibility for the collection of statistical data for the entire Ministry of Education. Data collection is also conducted by a number of offices and generally of a formative nature. (Wink, 1982, p. 304) . For example, The Specialized National Councils for Education, which reports to the president, has been identifying needs and solutions, making recommendations, and writing definitive

reports since 1974. The significance of these
reports is that they clearly identify needs and,
when the nature of the data collection is
considered, they provide a sound basis from which to
begin the accommodation of a foreign aid project
into the educational system. The Specialized Council
reports precede legislation because they have the
support of the executive office. But sometimes
foreign investors are not aware of these earlier
reports or they are not considered in follow-up
projects. For example, the American Project 4
reports, begun in Egypt with U.S. funding in the
1950's, involved the Instructional Technology Center
at Manshiet el Bakri. Visiting the facilities that
are still operating, one sees the necessity for
providing a follow-up budget for developing and
maintaining programs once began. Reports on Project
4 are not available in Egypt, but Egyptians who
participated 25 years earlier in program
implementation have less than optimistic views of
USAID as they witness planned expenditures for
projects which replicate earlier American efforts.

Another example of failure to read other
reports is found in the "Initial Project of USAID/E
Assistance--Recommendations in 1978 Vocational
Industrial Training in Egypt" which suggested the
design and implementation of a planning, evaluation,
research, and information office (like the
Educational Development Office of Project 4) at the
under-secretariat level, to conduct studies and
research and co-ordinate information-data needed
for managerial and operational decisions. This
report also included a fifth project which planned
the establishment of an Instructional Materials
Production Center (IMPC) like the Instructional
Center at Manshiet el Bakri of the 1950's. At the
proposed IMPC, the center would adapt instructional
materials validated in other countries and develop
new indigenous materials to accompany new
instructional methodologies and technologies. A new
center might not be constructed if Americans had
considered reports from the Point 4 programs or if
projects begun in the 1950's had been integrated
into later plans.

A second means of accommodating foreign aid is
to consider the administrative structure of the host
country. Committees and advisory councils make
recommendations to the ministers through a structure
which is hierarchical and vertical in its
communication. Policy making, planning and evaluation occur at the ministry level with

decentralization in the area of plan execution or implementation. (Wink, 1982, p. 200) Although the regions do make some planning decisions, regional decision making is defined by ministry guidelines and by resource limitations, as local jurisdictions have no regular source of revenue independent of the national government. (Wink, 1982, p. 201).

It should be remembered that Egypt is a country with a long history of centralized control and a tradition of "top down" decision making. There has, in the past, been little encouragement or reward for either initiative or decision making at the local level. In order to integrate the rural areas more actively into the process of national development, the present regime has embarked on a series of decentralization measures and has mandated the establishment of local councils which are to have a voice in matters concerning their own particular localities. (Wink, 1982, p. 203).

But for current formal administrative purposes, foreign aid projects are negotiated and decided upon by the central administrators who consult with others not necessarily a part of the formal organization.

As with many other administrative structures, the top administrator is a man who often has an even greater informal administrative system. His informal power is established through a network of personal relationships not clearly discernible. "The view of a man's self respect depends primarily on the respect others have for him." (Patai, 1976, p.310). This cultural value means that everyone is treated with the greatest respect. All projects must be cleared through many committees and administrators. Not to do so limits the respect accorded to each individual and makes the one in power appear to have poor character. For example, the request for a textbook change must be considered by all involved. A great many people might read and review the books. The common assumption might be that the books need to be changed and probably better books exist. But the disagreement of one person, regardless of the reasons, is unacceptable in the informal

administrative   system. The committees change and
the resolved arguments   are brought up by new
members. The adoption procedure is lengthened
considerably by this very important informal
administrative consideration. Committee members can
make a recommendation even though they have no more
authority than other members of the committee. But,
ultimately, only the   top administrator makes the
final decision.

Both the reward and the limitation of this
centralized   administration are that the top
administrator is critical to all functioning and is
the approval granting agent for the greatest number
of people. The administrators find   themselves
involved in all personal and professional
disagreements, in addition to policy making,
planning and evaluative decisions. They are the
center of all events and receive a great deal of
reward from significant personal   contributions to
the country. The limitation is that they are often
greatly overworked, dealing with both the routine
and the formal and informal requirements of the
office.

This personal power base is completely
understandable within   the existing system.
Institutions and policies change with the rapid
rise and fall of single individuals. When he was
replaced by Dr. Abdul Gaffar, in 1984, the Minister
of Education had held that post for 8 years, longer
than any other Minister of Education in recent
history. In order to establish personal power,
successors must alter or limit programs and plans
their predecessor began. Much of Sadat's popularity
was based upon destroying Nasser's police state.
Egyptian leaders are not always loyal to their
predecessors. Sadat, although Nasser's heir spent
much of his presidency dismantling Nasser's legacy.
(Reed, 1981, p. 184). But changing institutional
and political leadership cannot touch the power and
status of the family or friendships which rest on a
history of moral responsibility. Therefore, in
order to maintain stability in operations, personal
rather than institutional power is most reliable.

The resulting confusion to foreign investors is
observable. They sometimes have difficulty locating
people of informal influence as everyone is treated
with utmost respect. Their   conferences are
interrupted by people who to their perception
should not be received for efficiency's sake. And,
unknowingly, they may offend someone because they
are unaware of the informal communication patterns

which alter the reception of information. For example, perhaps the foreign agent is not himself the top administrator in a project and though he has certain delegated responsibilties, he may not, as a result of youth or rank, be perceived as the appropriate man to be conducting negotiations. Or coming from a less formal culture, he may behave appropriately for his country but not in the host country. And finally, coming on short visits does not allow the time necessary to relate to the Egyptians by developing a trusting friendship rather than institutional representative relationships. If Egyptians are to place commitment in a project, they are more confident when the representative has a personal relationship with them.

Knowledge about both the formal and informal administrative systems is a critical element in the accommodation of a program. Foreign aid programs which have operated outside of the educational administrative structure may differ in degree of centralization, and communication patterns. And certainly, as each country has its own cultural values, a difference in accepted informal communication patterns will exist. When a project is dominated by foreign project directors, technical assistants and support staff, the foreigners will communicate comfortably, accomplish tasks quickly and marvel at their own efficiency. And while they may be quickly established outside the centralized Egyptian educational system, they frequently disappear just as quickly. It seems necessary to the success of foreign aid programs for participants from different cultures to understand areas of difference which effect interphasing in both formal and informal administration.

One central area in which foreign aid is accommodated into the already existing system is the specialized training received in a foreign country. The difficulties posed to understaffed schools and universities when they must release personnel for overseas training are obvious. Many excellent candidates find themselves too central to their institutions to be given leave. However, specialized training has historically been both a reward for high achievement and an expedient manner of getting skilled workers. Problems of going to a foreign country, improving language skills if necessary and learning how to succeed in a different educational system are secondary to the accommodation difficulties the grantee faces upon return. The training has been completed many times at the sacrifice of separation from family and loss of professional advancement in terms of seniority in the native country, as the training period may vary from six months to several years. Young newly trained experts often return to the same job where they find newly acquired skills unnecessary or inappropriate and they must await promotion based upon the seniority system to place them in a position of authority. Thus, immediate rewards for personal sacrifice and increased knowledge may not materialize. Or, grantees may understand the accommodation difficulties they face upon returning to the system. In Egypt's socialistic economy, they cannot be fired and the training period is then perceived as a paid vacation and is treated as such. These conditions reduce the contribution of specialized training when accommodated and should instead be assimilated into the existing system.

The second integration option, assimilation of foreign aid projects, means a modification of, rather than an addition to processes and procedures which currently exist. Assimilation necessitates a significant investment in the infrastructure. For example, all innovation projects in the Ministry of Education are currently administered by committees which function apart from the hierarchical formal educational structures. (Wink, 1982, p. 305). In order for successful innovations to continue, they must be assimilated into the main administrative unit, which means in this case a redefinition of the existing Ministry of Education administrative guidelines.

In this more complex option, philosophical problems must be resolved before an innovation can be considered. Different is not necessarily better. In the last 10 years, the U.S. has emphasized science education, new math, bilingual education, women's equality, career education and more recently basic education and computer-assisted instruction. While computer assisted instruction is different, the appropriateness of implementing it in Egyptian schools, many of which have no electricity, is hardly feasible, let alone better. The lack of permanence of these trends in America and the increased funding for Egypt reflected in her political relationships rather than educational needs create resistence on the part of Egyptian education toward assimilating radically different approaches. A new leader more than likely will bring a new philosophy. Furthermore, given the environmental context, many innovations are not feasible. For example, what primary school teacher educated in a Western country could teach 50 children with no blackboards, textbooks, references or teaching supplies. And yet some Egyptian primary teachers are doing an excellent job under just such conditions. To assimilate a significantly different change into a functioning system is a risk. Success must be guaranteed in order to reject native-local experience efforts and culture. For the sake of stability, an innovation must be demonstrably better than the present process.

And the present process has been recognized as exceptional in the Middle East. Most of her 50 Middle Eastern universities were begun by Egyptians and some initially had Egyptian presidents. Sixty and sometimes as much as 90 percent of the teachers in the Gulf areas are Egyptian and they are in demand. (Masellus, B., Jarrar, S., personal interview 1983). In 1978 alone, 30,000 Egyptian teachers and professors were employed in Arab and African countries. And over 50,000 Arabs, Africans and Asians were receiving an education in Egypt. (Jarrar, S., personal interview 1984). Both these factors demonstrate the success of methodologies employed in the present educational system. Therefore, providing funding for educational projects that differ significantly from the current processes do not recognize the effectiveness of the existing system.

Assimilating a different procedure, whether producing a product, training, or altering the entire system, involve phases of acceptance and implementation. Orientation, preparation, use, refinement, integration and renewal are components in the assimilation process. (Hall, 1975, p. 52). Instruction can be provided as preparation but it must also include instruction in the resulting changes in the total system. For example, a teacher can be told how to utilize problem-solving in the classroom. But she must also be made aware of the discrepancies between the philosophy behind problem solving and the beliefs which reinforce continued use of former teaching strategies. Perhaps her culture has placed higher status upon the theoretical than practical aspects of education and as a result, she possesses a belief system which reinforces the lecture format. If she is lecturing a large portion of the time, she must understand the relationship between lecturing and

133

problem-solving teaching techniques, the necessary changes in her role, and the participation process of the students. Furthermore, if she is to change, she must be given the resources and facilities to make the adoption of the new technique economical, less difficult and educationally rewarding to the students and to herself.

The context, the change and the need for change are factors to be understood and resolved in the orientation and preparation stages. Most proposals stop at this point. Little support is provided for monitoring the mechanical usage of the new technique, developing a routine, refinement of the process and finally integration and renewal. On a very small scale, the purchase of equipment and instruction in its usage do not ensure that it will be used, that later personnel will be trained or that equipment will be repaired when inoperative. These maintenance and follow-up components are critical aspects of the delivery system. Each assimilation phase profiles a different decision point that the participants must understand in order to thoroughly assimilate the innovation or change into the existing system. When larger projects such as Basic Education or technical education interphase with the existing systems, the stages of assimilation become even more critical if continued utilization is to be ensured.

Foreign aid to education must either be accommodated or assimilated into the existing educational system. And because of the centralization of the Egyptian administrative structure, beginning stages of policy-making and planning and report writing are more easily accomplished than implementation, maintenance, and follow-up which take place on site. More substantial emphasis must be placed upon developing an infrastructure--especially at the lower admin-levels. This is not easily accomplished in Egypt as a history of delegation of authority has not predominated within both formal and informal administrative structures. The successful accomplishments of foreign aid projects must consider the accommodation or assimilation of the project components within the existing educational system. Not to do so is to risk that the financial aid becomes the end and not the means of developing the existing educational systems.

The importance of these considerations have been clearly lacking in English language instruction in Egypt. In 1980, a proposal was written by Group 7, an American needs assessment team, visiting Egypt to determine how American developmental assistance could improve English competency of Egyptians. The short-range goal from the American perspective was to prepare participants to meet USAID language requirements for Peace Fellowships and other American sponsored exchange programs. The focus was to provide adults with English skills rather than accommodating or assimilating the training into the existing educational system. Selected participants would have to be a product of that educational system, but its infrastructure of teachers, inspectors, curriculum, and materials would not be altered.

The Egyptians, while recognizing the need for English language training, had a history of the British to consider. With British occupation, large numbers of British teachers came to Egypt and developed a strong English program in the governmental and specialized English language schools. Under Nasser, the British teachers left and a concerted effort was made to translate English textbooks into Arabic. In fact, from 1960 to 1968, the translation of English technical books into Arabic was supported by American PL480 funds. (Garrison, 1969 p.3). University tests and textbooks remain in English in many professional schools, but classroom instruction in medicine, science, agriculture, engineering, and some social sciences is in Arabic. The result is university graduates can read and write English, but do not necessarily demonstrate fluency in speaking or understanding spoken English.

With President Sadat's open door policy, the demand for English in both public and private sector jobs reasserted itself. Some Egyptian government positions, such as postal service and customs, made English competency a prerequisite for placement. And if one wanted to leave government jobs and get positions in the better paying private sector, English was generally required. Egyptian businessmen and government officials found English was the language of the international community. By the end of the 1970's, English had again become useful in both academic and professional life.

The need was established and universities, secondary schools, and even pre-schools felt the pressure. According to the director of the English Language Center at Cairo University, of the 75,000 students enrolled in 1975, 25,000 needed English language training. But the university system was restricted by a Supreme Council of Universities policy that placed language instruction under the jurisdiction of the English departments, which have a traditional emphasis on literature. Therefore, instructors in language classes have training in literature, but not necessarily in linguistics and teaching English as a foreign language. (USAID Proposal, 1980, p.4). To alleviate this problem, the Supreme Council of Universities intends to establish five model language centers in Cairo, Assuit, Ain Shams, Alexandria, and Tanta universities. (Member of Supreme Council of Universities, personal interview, 1982). The Cairo University program is in place and Tanta University provides both a university sponsored English language program and an additional tuition charging program in the Faculty of Commerce conducted in co-operation with the Department of Public Service at American University in Cairo.

On the secondary level, foreign language schools, many of which provide more hours of English language instruction, are in demand. Conversely, schools whose curriculum includes one or two hours of English instruction per week cannot prepare students for university work. Students in secondary schools do not have a strong English background because Law 123, enacted in 1956, abolished English from the subjects taught at the primary stage. The law was prompted by the lack of English language teachers, anti-British feelings, and the pedagogical assumption that language instruction was more appropriate at the preparatory level. The final secondary thanawaya ama exam does not reflect the need for English language as a student may fail the English component and still not significantly affect the total passing score. (Principal, Ramses College for Girls, personal interview, 1983). But the student who does fail to master English will not be successful in the university and will not be able to get a job in the private sector. Students understand this fact and the increasing enrollments at A.U.C., the British Council, and the numerous, small, private English language schools reflect students' motivation to improve their economic and academic skills.

And finally, technical and scientific instruction in the secondary schools and the higher institutes require English to access new technological advances or even understand assembly and repair manuals on foreign-made machinery. Much of the technology in computer and other rapidly

changing technological fields is in English.
Translation of such information and-or instructional
manuals means both the training process and the
communication of up-to-date methodologies is
lengthened. Furthermore, many technical experts
train in English even if it is not their native
language, and those who wish to go on exchange
programs in many foreign countries must also know
English.

In order to improve the educational imbalance
in technical training, university exchanges, and
enable students to obtain private sector jobs, the
Egyptians must improve English language instruction.
In order for American technical and developmental
assistance programs to be efficiently implemented,
candidates must have English competency. Both
parties are in agreement regarding the need, but the
American proposed plan ignores the Egyptian
educational system. Instead it proposes to create
parallel functions, neither accommodated nor
assimilated into the Egyptian context.

The 1980 Group 7 American proposal recommended
the following: participant training programs,
counterpart (those who will remain in Egypt)
training programs, technical assistance to non-
profit private and public sector organizations to
develop English language training programs,
contracting with an "appropriate organization" to
provide technical assistance. "The appropriate
organization should conduct such activities as
providing general workshops for co-ordinators of EFL
programs in Egypt, ongoing seminars for co-
ordinators in the areas of teacher training,
curriculum development and the use of audio-visual
equipment as resources in EFL, and evaluation of
training. The external organization should also
provide in-service training and curriculum
development for specific areas." (USAID, 1980, p.3).
All of these recommendations were directed toward
creating a separate English language training
program with the short-range goal of preparing
participants to meet USAID requirements.

Along with the innovations in the Ministry of
Education that are not part of the institutionalized
administrative structure, these separate training
programs risk disappearance and-or failure. The
recommendations begin, as Mohammed Ali began, with a
top-down or pyramid development. He soon discovered
there was a need to build an infrastructure to
support this pyramid. The same will be true with
English language instruction if it follows the

proposed model. The length of time required to
master English, even with rudimentary beginnings,
cannot be provided in short intensive periods of
instruction as indicated in the American University
in Cairo-English Language Institute report:

> "During the current year, more and
> more participants have come with
> lower proficiency scores, some as
> low as 30. This has caused some
> problems with student progress and
> motivation. It is difficult for
> students who come with ALIGU scores
> in the 30's to make the necessary
> gains to reach 70 in eight weeks.
> Average gains were 20 points for an
> eight-week cycle. There is no reason,
> however, to expect this kind of gain
> for students at the lower
> proficiency level." (Government
> Document, Intensive English AID
> Report, 1978).

And as the base for selecting Peace Fellowship
and other exchange candidates broadens into
management and middle-management levels, it seems
unlikely that even the short term intensive training
at the top of the pyramid will be sufficient.
Therefore, it makes sense that the USAID proposal
should consider building the English language
infrastructure within the existing educational
system. The first step toward improving English
language instruction on the secondary level has
been taken by the Egyptians. A small USAID grant
was spent to modify the English component of the
thanawaya ama exam through adding a proficiency
component. According to the former director of
English language inspectors, Dr. Guirgis Rashidi,
this alteration directed classroom instruction
toward conversation and greater usage of language
structures.
However, admission to the participant and
counterpart training taking place at American
University in Cairo has not considered the English
thanawaya ama exam scores which all candidates must
have taken. Instead, the ALIGUE is administered as
a pre- and post-test. The ALIGUE is not in essay
test format familiar to Egyptians. Further, the
ALIGUE is normed on a culturally different
population and has a poor ability to measure
English competency at lower skill levels. Since

the test provides no placement information, individual program placement and exit tests must be administered to potential candidates who meet AUC entrance requirements. For example, low scoring participants and counterpart candidates take the hour-long ALIGUE screening test and then other AUC exams before entrance into the English programs. Co-operation on the English component of the thanawaya ama exam would simplify the testing and candidate selection process, and support existing secondary school testing procedures. Enormous USAID administrative expense and effort goes into scheduling and evaluating a separate testing program which yields results only meaningful to USAID administration.

There is a necessity to rethink English language training and testing. Instructors and administrators involved in selecting participants are concerned with the blanket testing regulations contained in AID Handbook 10 which require minimum ALIGU test scores (which differ slightly for academic and non-academic participants). Egyptian officials who are aware of the testing pocedures are also critical of the methodology, terming it culture-bound.

The second English language proposal recommendation was to provide technical assistance to non-profit public and private organization in Egypt to develop separate English language training programs. Aside from the conflict with Egyptian universities that are planning to increase their programs, this support will further reduce the pool of competent teachers available for government schools, many of whom prefer working in private language academies paying up to L.E.10 an hour for instructors. Egyptians have rejected the USAID proposal to staff proposed training centers with Peace Corps volunteers. Given the lack of success with the Princeton-in-Asia staffed English language programs in the 1930's, this rejection was warranted. However, the need for English training must extend beyond major cities to cities where English language teachers are not prevalent. The alternative of placing American English language teachers in outlying areas is a major expenditure which does not guarantee the ability to educate without expected facilities, resources, and equipment. The technical assistance to external agencies is viable in Cairo and Alexandria, but also competitive with rather than supportive of Egyptian educational plans.

The USAID proposal also recommended that an external organization will provide workshops and on-going seminars for co-ordinators in teacher training, curriculum development, and use of AV equipment and resources in EFL and evaluation training. These sugestions appear to be replications of functions of Egyptian faculties of education or teacher training institutes. Since these existing units are not included in the proposed plan, it is difficult to conceive of who will be the recipients of this training and how it can be delivered to rural Egypt. Competent and not so competent English teachers are currently employed by the schools and are earning additional money tutoring and working for private language institutes.

The teacher shortage is acute in Cairo and even worse in outlying areas, especially in English. The proposal to staff such centers from the Peace Corps has been unacceptable to Egyptians. A second suggestion, that of placing Fulbright professors in linguistics in rural universities, would not provide continuity even if there were enough such professors willing to live in rural, predominantly Arabic-speaking areas. A third alternative, that of placing qualified Egyptians taken from universities and government schools, would further restrict existing programs if there were enough qualified Egyptians.

Potential teachers would be unable or unwilling to leave the security they have with government positions, for new language centers unless the pay was better. The more likely candidates for teacher training would need English language training rather than use of AV resources as suggested in the proposal. Furthermore, new curriculum and approaches have not been historically well received. For a number of years, the Alexander English language series was used in the schools and finally abandoned as the audio-lingual presentation did not match the teachers' background and preference. Furthermore, the failure to order expensive teachers' manuals that accompanied the series affected instruction. Teachers, overworked and sometimes lacking knowledge, did not have the time to devise a communication methodology for presenting the material. As a result, they would have students repeat after them, make up sentences, and memorize and copy English from the text. The books were abandoned for an older text which was more compatible with teacher experience and perceived needs. In short, neither the proposed participants nor content of seminars is feasible or appropriate for the existing situation.

Even the methodology of presenting seminars or ongoing training has not produced results when tried. Workshops and seminars are a university concept and not necessarily applicable to the improvement of classroom teaching, although generally enjoyable. "A four day workshop seminar on language testing was conducted on behalf of the Ministry of Education, hosted by the American University in Cairo in the spring of 1982. Several American, British, and Egyptian participants contributed by speaking and leading discussion groups. All senior inspectors and a majority of the inspector generals attended. Their transportation, per diem, and workshop refreshments were provided under the grant. A formal evaluation form was prepared and distributed to all participants. Overall evaluation was extremely high, many participants requesting the workshop to be repeated on a regular basis." (Henning, 1983, p. 1). As this report suggests, there is no linkage between seminar presentation and testing improvement or actual classroom instruction, although everyone enjoyed themselves. The hypothesis is that the classroom instruction will change as a result of the seminar but this hypothesis was not measured.

Assuming that center facilities could be built or located and English teachers found, the network for establishing support facilities does not exist. "With respect to other mission training needs, specifically technical assistance to the public and private sectors in developing or strengthening EFL programs, there are a number of Cairo-based educational institutions which may be called upon to provide such assistance. Among these are the Center for the Development of English Teaching (CEDELT) at Ain Shams University, the various English language programs at the American University in Cairo, and the Fulbright Commission." (USAID Proposal, 1980, p.9). It should be noted that each of these Cairo-based educational institutions is not integrated into the main educational administrative base of the Egyptian educational system; CEDELT, as May 1983 had 15 students enrolled and was located at Ain Shams University, not affiliated with the language instruction at the university. American University in Cairo is the only private university in Egypt, and the Fulbright Commission is a support service facilitator providing housing, mail delivery, and

141

transportation, mostly in Cairo. None of these educational units have the infrastructure themselves to provide any type of educational assistance to newly formed training centers. The lack of a support system has prevented the American University in Cairo from opening a successful branch campus outside of Cairo, although three significant attempts were made in Suez, Tanta, and Malta.

Even when programs are funded, Egyptians may refuse to participate as evidenced by the participant reduction in September of 1983. The counterpart training, which was conducted at AUC, was eliminated by the Egyptian responsible for sending candidates. As a result, American teachers who had expected contracts were eliminated in July. The expected population of 160 students was eliminated in the D.P.S. Program ($22,300 out of a total grant of $948,476) and the other two training programs sharply reduced. As with the CEDELT program, ministry officials who were involved can and do prevent students from attending, effective programs from continuing, and allocated money from being spent.

The logical recourse is to work within the existing educational framework. This was never a consideration of the USAID proposal. The proposal even recommended that no attempt should be made to up-grade existing English language institutes for the purpose of increasing facilities for USAID training.

In 1985, there was no evidence of any of the plans outlined in the USAID proposal of 1980. The need for English language training still existed but implementation was based upon suggestions which neither assimilated or accommodated themselves into the Egyptian system. Fourteen foreign master's level English language specialists were hired on two-year contracts to teach at rural universities beginning in September of 1984. It is hoped that their salary of $21,000 will motivate them to stay for an extended period even though their salary will create difficulties with lower paid Egyptian superiors and co-workers. (Bowers, personal interview, 1984). It is apparent from both the educational goals of the country and the economic needs of the people that English language instruction in its broadest sense is necessary. The proposed American plan discusses short-range train- ing in order to improve the selection process for the admininstration of its own grants. The corollary is that Egyptians will benefit from

improved language skills. A wider vision is
needed--one which either accommodates or assimilates
itself into the existing conditions in the Egyptian
educational institutions and aids in the development
of an infrastructure to support the continuation of
current programs on an improved basis.
   Two significant factors are apparent in foreign
investment in Egypt. When a country lacks the
infrastructure to disseminate financial allocations,
little observable change is made. The money serves
to enrich those at the top of the administrative
structure, but little reaches those for whom the
money is intended. Secondly, when resources are
allocated to projects which are not compatible
within the educational procedures and goals of the
country, the projects are accepted but not
implemented. As illustrated by American aid to
education, those projects which represent Western
values have been subtly ignored by the Egyptians...a
statement for their own cultural integrity and a
process generally unrecognized by foreign investors.

CHAPTER VIII REFERENCES

Bowers, Roger. (1980-1981). "Summary of Evaluation Recommendations 2/80 and Notes on Their Status," Center for Developing English Language Teaching, July.

Childs, William. (1978). "Final Report, Recommendations and Observations," University Textbook Program Component of the University Instructional Material and Library Project, International Publishing Services, McLean, Virginia.

Government Document.(1978). "Intensive English Training for AID Mission Participant Trainees," August.

Hall, Gene, et al. (1975). "Levels of Use of the Innovation: A Framework for Analyzing Innovation Adoption," Journal of Teacher Education, Vol. XXVI, No. 1, Spring.

Henning, Grant. (1983). English Language Testing Grant Interim Report. April 18.

Hall, T. J. "Innovation in Education". (1978). Unpublished research paper from the University of Texas, presented at Texas ASCD Conference, San Antonio, Texas.

Masellus, Byron, and Garrar, Samir. (1983). "Education in the Middle East," Praeser Press, New York, New York.

Patai, Raphael. (1978). "The Arab Mind," Houghton Mifflin Co., Boston.

Reed, Stanley. (1981-82). "Dateline Cairo: Shaken Pillar," Foreign Policy, 45.

USAID. (1980). "Document for Development of Related English Language Training, Needs and Resources," Egypt, No. JOU ES-AAA 190.

Wink, Karen. (1982). "A Description and Analysis of the Process Process of Educational Planning in Egypt," Unpublished doctoral dissertation, University of Southern California, Los Angeles, California.

CHAPTER IX

CONCLUSIONS AND RECOMMENDATIONS

Education provides both security and improved ability of its participants to survive in their environment. Because of the socialistic economy, Egypt's graduates find guaranteed jobs do not pay well and they are forced to take second and third jobs in order to cope with inflation and family needs. Security and survival abilities have not improved for Egyptian graduates. In contrast, the goals of education from the beginning of Egypt's history have not changed--to transfer practical and cultural knowledge to its citizenry, a knowledge which enables them to become productive as individuals in the society and appreciative of the culture. The problem has been the adoption of one goal for one segment of society to the exclusion of the other throughout periods of recent history. During Mohammed Ali's rule, technical, practical education was emphasized for a select group of Egyptians. The British occupation which followed again provided select Egyptians with technical governmental, and bureaucratic education. From 1920-1952 there was the need for raising the literacy of the people in order to impart cultural values with the neglect of technological education. From 1956 to the present, technical and cultural education both have been paramount. Since the early 1980's both technical and primary education are being addressed within the framework of a unified educational system. But financial allocations have resulted in a foreign investment in technical education and an Egyptian emphasis on social education, contributing to a divided society.

The cause of the educational dichotomy in Egypt today is that legal, cultural, and social knowledge is based upon the Koran while industrial,

145

commercial, and technological knowledge is based upon the blending of many specialized and sometimes foreign sources. Cultural knowledge is mastered through memorization and recitation of the Koran, the unifying source of social knowledge. Technical and practical knowledge cannot be securely mastered when students apply the same approach and recite theorems or scientific axioms. One must be able to apply memorized scientific concepts to situations which are undefined and unexplained. Both sources of knowledge bring comprehension of the world in which one lives. However, the source of social knowledge is absolute while technical knowledge has brought change and social insecurity with its acquisition. The conflict in the current educational system can be traced to the religious and secular power struggle within Egyptian society. On one hand are the religious leaders with a history of representing absolute knowledge to the populace and the government. On the other hand are the secular leaders with their specialized technical knowledge.

Currently, a debate is taking place between fundamentalist and liberal leaders of the religious community about how to integrate the two ways of knowing. This is summarized by the Islamic scholar Taha Hussain in his <u>Preface to Four Soliloquies with Allah and the Religious Debate</u>.

> The case to be seriously discussed can be summed up as follows: some religious thinkers want to have the sole right to shape the mentality of whole a nation on the basis of the only religious books that are available to them regardless of any up-to-date addition. They also refuse to allow others to lead and shape the mentality of the people based upon science and contemporary culture without supervising such leadership in spite of the wide gap between what is fixed in religions and what should change with change in time and place.

> Scientists and thinkers realize that the shaping of a nations' mentality should be the job of all the human elements that are based upon man's mental and sensitive activities such as religious belief, scientific thoughts, literature, art, and culture. The culture of our forefathers is merely a result of human minds and hearts

that have lived a civilization that is different from ours.

We should not restrict ourselves within the limits of those past ideals alone and allow them to chain our thinking or become a limit beyond which we cannot move. This making us turn for hundreds of years in a vicious circle around one past era as if Islam were not fit except for this one age with its thoughts and circumstances. We cannot build all our ideas around the first Islamic era and forget that Islam is fit for every age and true and flexible enough for life and progress anywhere and anytime. God is bigger, his science is wider, his mercy deeper and his forgiveness broader. (Hussain, 1984).

This debate is a part of what C.P. Snow wrote of in Two Cultures, and has more recently concerned Toffler and Naisbit. But the Egyptian educational process is not constructed on a flexible foundation. It's security is based in a process of memorization which enables one to master a large number of facts expediently. Otherwise, the country must adopt a curriculum and testing process which is not and cannot be encouraged in the present social system. It would require alteration and development of the inspector, teacher, methodology, and educational infrastructure, and there would have to be a guarantee that such a reorganization would be beneficial for the society as a whole. The high incidence of divorce, crime, and interpersonal abuse in Western culture as communicated by their press, movies, and TV does not speak well for the social benefits of this flexible educational process--a system which teaches the questioning of absolutes threatening the stability of Egypt's religious leadership. There can be little tolerance for providing an education in how to make choices when knowledge of the best manner in which to live has been provided. This certainty of knowledge enables fundamentalists to feel secure in their actions and encourages conflict with secular change.

Before the 1950's the society had been static and predictable. Each knew his place, and the behavior and the accepted values which would gain him respect within his ascribed status. The landowners controlled the people, told them when to vote, when to pay taxes. Furthermore, the landowners took care of the workers when they were sick or infirmed. And life revolved around the Nile. But with the 1950's came the Aswan Dam which altered the flow of the Nile and increased the dynamism of society represented by technology. Since socialism, all men have had a right to land. Ignorance was shameful and the government would take care of its people. The dependency of the people was transferred from the landowners to the government. The changes were social, economic and political. Education became the disseminator of these changes.

But within the secular educational system, there existed a cultural vacuum. Teachers were the cultural role models but they were poorly paid, poorly trained and overworked. They could do little more than maintain control in overcrowded classrooms that lacked equipment, facilities and sometimes electricity. As representatives of the dynamic future, they offered little vision to their students in how to proceed with their lives.

Furthermore, the teachers had difficulty in establishing respect when some were the least successful graduates of the preparatory schools and were from lower social strata than some of their students. The cultural values must then come from the family which had been reduced in its power economically and sometimes politically by the system of informers that existed under Nasser and concomitant reduction of the family's ability to provide economic support. So while cultural values were in transition, the communication of these values to the students resulted in confusion. The working of the land did not provide respect and going to school did not enable them to acquire better paying jobs, thus improving their lives. They were a product of their educational system but the knowledge imparted did not aid them in knowing how to live in their changing society or how to earn a better living. The importance of providing cultural education in the values and integrity of the society increased in significance in this dynamic society. The ultimate goal of science as a means of improving man's life had not been adequately communicated in the conflict between technology and the established social values.

One means of retaining security has been to emphasize cultural, social and religious values of the past, and resist change, but the severity of the technological problems threatens the country. Overcrowding in the cities and environmental pollution are critical and all suffer as support systems strain to maintain the existing and expected population. Societal conflict was increased by environmental and economic conditions which threatened survival.

Egypt's economic situation is especially precarious because less than 4 percent of her land is arable; the rest is desert. A population of about 40 million is concentrated in the Nile Valley and the delta region, north of Cairo, and this population is growing by more than one million a year--one of the highest rates of increase in the world. The urban rate of growth of 3 to 4 percent a year strains the government's ability to provide the amenities of life: housing, water, electricity, education, and transportation.

Cairo is the epitome of rampant urbanization. The city and its environs contain an estimated 9 million inhabitants, most of whom live in overcrowded, poor quarters; thousands live in the cemetery City of the Dead. Sewage disposal is a massive problem. The water supply system requires increasing chlorination; and those who can afford it drink only bottled water. Electrical blackouts are commonplace in the old city where more than three-fourths of the city-dwellers live.

Deterioration in public transportation has caused disturbances and violence, particularly on trains from Cairo to Helwan. Buses are the main mode of transportation, but they are sorely inadequate, notwithstanding additions from Iran and the United States. The fare is minimal, but it is unlikely that many people pay, because of the sardine-like packing of commuters who mount and dismount through windows as well as doors. The main arteries are clogged, and the several hours

required to get from one part of the
city to another seriously affect
business and   personal appointments.

The government's discretionary spending is limited. The military budget
takes 20 to 25 percent of revenues.
Another 25 percent goes for
subsidies, which   have mushroomed:
in 1972, the government spent about
$20 million on subsidies; by 1975, as
a result of   escalating food prices
on world markets, the total   had
risen to almost $900 million; in
1978, the total   may exceed $1.7
billion. The price of bread is
roughly the same today as it was in
1939 (though the   loaf is bit
smaller and coarser); the government
maintains this artificial price
through a subsidy of $600 million
to $700 million a year intended to
cushion the poor from the impact of
rising inflation.   Egypt imports
between $2 billion and $3 billion
dollars more in goods than she
exports. In recent   years, the
deficits have been made up mainly by
loans and grants from Arab countries
and the United States. (Benoit, 1978,
p. 817).

The society can not easily afford to allow
education to take a slow evolutionary course as in
the past. The social problems facing the country
require immediately an educated populace who can
utilize sophisticated and innovative technological
solutions.   As the educational system had been
unable to respond rapidly to pressures of increased
population, foreign technologists were imported
increasing the divisions in the society.
Even the Egyptians who are graduates of
technical institutions had a difficult time
interphasing into scientific and commercial projects
as a result of their method of instruction. It is
one thing to be able to recite a theorem, quote a
passage from a textbook, or memorize the words of
the teacher for delivery on an exam. It is quite
another to be able to apply theory, equation, or
rule of physics in a practical application. The
required skills are different and extend beyond the

memorization level which the Egyptian graduate has thoroughly mastered.

This comprehension and application skill is not a necessary component of the instructional process. If the Egyptian engineer, architect or chemist does not have an adequate training manual or a sufficiently competent trainer in his place of employment, his ability to translate and demonstrate his acquired knowledge is limited by his own motivation and ingenuity. While the technical graduate has received training, the process of instruction has severely restricted his ability to produce and thus contribute to society.

RECOMMENDATIONS

From the perspective of the developing country, Egypt has invested a great deal of effort to graduate technical workers. If the technical workers are unable to perform, the effort is difficult to justify. It might be to the country's advantage to bring technical experts from abroad as Muhammed Ali did rather than train their own scientists and technicians who are unable to solve developmental problems efficiently. Technological expertise is a source of power and leadership, one which Egyptians must often relinquish to foreigners. The importance of addressing technological problems has been emphasized by the requests for development assistance to education, the largest portion of which has gone toward scientific and technical education. The irony is that this expenditure may not result in the quality of graduate which would be possible if the delivery of content were altered.

The solution to effective technological education lies not so much in the talent of the students, which will always vary, as in the preparation of the teachers in the delivery of content. Teacher training must be paramount, beginning with instructors trained in relating absolutes to practical needs. The educational system as it is presently constituted facilitates the memorization of facts and theory independent of the classroom teacher on all levels of education. It is not necessary for the teachers to drill students in facts. What is necessary is that the teachers build bridges between the facts as memorized from the books and the application of these facts to present conditions. Current and future textbooks do not and cannot accomplish transfer as the writers neither know present problems nor can they predict future applications a priori. The theory as it is currently taught is necessary but often unusable.

Secondly, the examinations should test application in addition to factual knowledge. The current testing structure is the only feasible means of maintaining quality control and assuring that the curriculum has been mastered. In the case of English language instructions, the exam was altered from an exam which could be passed by memorization to an application exam. Predictably, the instruction in the classrooms changed toward understanding and usage of English on the part of the teacher and the students. Necessary technological content, in theory, exists as the scientific and technological textbooks are either Arabic translations or original textbooks. And as classroom instruction is directed toward passing national exams, the tests themselves require modification in order to alter instruction.

But when teachers have minimal or inadequate training, they rely heavily upon the textbook. Another emphasis must then be on training the teachers to use the textbook effectively. If this is not done, teachers will present the material in the same way as they were taught as they have no other model. While teacher training will have to be repeated with textbook changes, the rewards of such on-site training will far outweigh the cost of current efforts to totally retrain 139,000 primary and some secondary teachers.

Furthermore, the textbooks themselves should be modified to consider the conditions in most classrooms. Supplementary reference material is simply not available and should therefore be given in the text or teacher manual. Physical equipment does not exist in many cases and so more practical methods of conducting experiments should be provided. All visuals should be included in the textbook if they exist. And finally, students should be given the principles they are learning and applications of these principles in problems and drill. The teacher cannot be expected to make all these transitions when knowledge of subject matter and teaching techniques are not strong. And most importantly, the text should be constructed so that the student can master the transfer process independent of the teacher as it is more than likely his parents or a tutor will be helping him.

The major thrust of education in Egypt in the past 30 years has been to increase the enrollment and resources. The second thrust has been to provide practical skills and technical knowledge enabling the graduates to meet the country's developmental needs and to provide them with marketable skills. There has been a consistent emphasis on technical training in the past 30 years and currently the World Bank projects have focused solely on this area. The machinery and buildings are financed but the teacher training and texts have been so narrow in focus that only a specific skill has been taught, neglecting cultural and societal knowledge. If this is not considered as a component of the technical training programs, technical education will serve no better purpose than it did under Mohammed Ali or the British. The graduates will not have a cultural foundation and thus lack a basis from which to integrate secular and religious factions in the country. This is not to say that cultural education is ignored in the technical high schools administered by the Ministry of Labor. However the specificity of the materials and the accelerated teacher training program makes this a danger to consider.

It is no secret what makes an effective educational system: strong administrative leadership at the local and national level, shared goals, high expectations, parental involvement, competent and committed teachers and motivated students. Egyptian students are initially motivated as they view education as a means for social status and security. They become disenchanted when they find the government positions awaiting them in the public sector, while secure, pay significantly less than the private sector jobs. It is not unusual to find a young girl taking a secretarial certificate course while remaining in a university in order to insure that she has the status of a university degree and potentially the money from a private sector job. Furthermore, competent and committed teachers are necessary. The L.E.50-60 a primary or secondary teacher earns does not enable him or her to survive. So they tutor, drive taxis before and after school or leave for more lucrative positions inside the country. The parental involvement in school is overwhelming particularly in the area of tutoring their children. It is almost as if the children attend school but the responsibility for their achievement rests with the parents. Even a poor man must find the money to have a son's test grade raised and buy military uniforms for other sons in school. (Abdul Karim, Doorman, 1983, personal interview) The commitment of the parents reflects the high expectations they have from education. The

153

goals shared by parents and students alike are that
education will enable them to lead a better life
economically and personally.

And, at this time, the educational system is
overwhelmed by the country's greatest resource--
people. One out of every seven Egyptians is in some
educational institution--a testimony to both the
youthfulness of the population and the effort to
educate them. The Egyptian people are the country's
untapped resource. As a people, they are kind,
co-operative and respectful of others and of
authority. Both cultural values and encouragement of
their families makes them eager to learn and this
quest for knowledge is a challenge the country must
meet--not only to provide them with access to
education but also with skills and values which
prepare the young to meet the challenges facing
their country.

The leaders who are directing the educational
process are primarily at the national level. Local
principals and school officials have little to say
about the curriculum, national exams or discipline.
How much can be done by central educational
administration when qualified local administrators
are not given the power to appropriately adapt
administrative policy is a significant question.
There is no academic administration training
available in any university. This means that all
school administrators currently employed have had to
learn management, budgeting and building operation
on site. There are some excellent local
administrators who were able to acquire this
knowledge on their own. There is no reason to
believe that other administrators might not prove
just as efficient if they were given some support
and guidance through on site training. The
administrators, teachers and textbooks are the
infrastructure of the educational system and they
have been neglected in the national education
perspective.

The problem of education in Egypt and to a
greater or lesser degree in all countries has been
the applicability of skills learned in school to the
survival needs of the individual and the country.
Presently, knowledge acquired through education has
not enabled some individuals to reap sufficient
economic rewards due to the employment process, the
need to use English, and the competition resulting
from overpopulation. For example, even the most
intelligent, and most highly educated physicians
find it difficult to afford clinics, work for low

salaries in the government as required, or extract high fees from poor clients. Their efficiency is thwarted by the social, economic, and political structure. On the other hand, the society cannot operate efficiently without skilled agriculturalists, doctors, plumbers and mechanics. Graduates of these disciplines who are unable to satisfactorily apply their skills in present day situations meet no needs--even if the number graduated meets the number required in the country.

The present problems of education in Egypt are painful, immediate and potentially explosive. They are painful as effort is expended on all levels by and for students who are generally highly motivated. The documented wastage of drop-outs, misplacement in occupations, and graduates who are unable to perform is painful to both the graduates and society as a whole. The immediacy of the problems have been emphasized by the reorganization plan which is comprehensive and effects all levels of primary and secondary education. In this effort, the 17 multi-targeted programs were all scheduled to begin in the 1981-82 academic year. These programs began without sufficient funding, underscoring the commitment of the government and the seriousness with which the educational issues are perceived. Education cannot be denied to all who view it as their right. And yet, when they become aware of the limited rewards and usefulness of their knowledge, they may become disenchanted with the current social system. In a country where a large portion of the population is under 25, a poorly educated or dissatisfied segment of the population provides a dangerous threat to the stability of the country.

When society is dynamic rather than static, knowledge consists in its translation from the textbook or source to application and the critical evaluation of its appropriateness to societal needs. The students, therefore, should be examined on the application of mastered facts to the functions of society. Unfortunately, this form of education in Egypt has been associated with foreign schools and hence foreign occupation and values. Egyptian nationalism has meant that education remains static in its classroom presentation which has undermined the effectiveness of what students learn when validated through employment competency or the ability to address developmental problems. The tolerance for ambiguity as a result of a number of choices and a number of equally possible solutions will require a new definition and acquisition of

knowledge. The resolution of today's educational
conflict is to be found in expanding not only the
access and curriculum as has been done in the past
but expanding the definition and process of
acquiring knowledge.

The resolution of Egypt's educational problems
do not, however, require drastic institutional
change. The problems have been identified and
documented and funding has been solicited. The
solutions do not relate to a lack of vision or
resources as Egyptians for the last 100 years has
been moving in the appropriate direction to find
solutions. The emphasis of education in the last 100
years has been to increase enrollment and to thereby
increase the literacy and the ease with which
societal needs and values can be transmitted. In the
final analysis, education in Egypt has identified
goals, integrated them into one educational system,
and targeted further areas of expansion and
interest. She needs only to develop her teachers,
pedagogy, examinations, and administrative
infrastructure. Primarily by altering the method of
presenting the curriculum, the schools can prepare
graduates to enter society and adjust to change. The
cultural values and content need not be destroyed
but they will be questioned. Taha Hussain indicated
the religion would be strong enough to endure such
inquiry. The instructional method, if altered, would
integrate both systems, secular and religious, into
an education appropriate for all Egyptians. Security
would be maintained and survival enhanced as the
knowledge that is taught flows out of the classroom
and into the country.

The overwhelming need of the Egyptian is to be
secure and survive in a society which has become
dynamic rather than static. The educational system
with its history of elite and populace divergence
has created a country whose people are in conflict
with themselves. On one hand are those who have been
trained toward obedience and conformity to the
religious and cultural heritage of the past. "When
stripped down to its bare bones, the bulk of the
Islamic militants are intensely nationalistic, from
middle-class backgrounds, and have modern educa-
tions." (Ibrahim, 1981, p. 94). This population
labels as "foreign" changes in social values and
behavior which threaten the security of the past. On
the other hand are those who have been trained
toward an expression of change and, for want of
another word, technology. These graduates have been
supported by the World Bank, USAID, and other

foreign sources which have provided alternate models
survival. And between these two groups are the
Egyptian agrarian and urban poor, accounting for
Egypt's increasing economic subsidies and population
increase. It is the education of the poor which at
this time is receiving the bulk of the attention
through Basic Education and other educational
reorganization plans. The education of the poor will
determine the future stability of the country. The
education the poor receive must be closely examined
as to its fit into the economic and social needs of
the country. It must prepare them with security,
pride in their heritage and confidence in the
usefulness of their skills in facing the future. It
must deny neither the past nor the future in its
translation of knowledge to the world in which the
young Egyptian must live. Egypt's conflicts are not
yet over nor are their resolution in sight. And only
when the reconciliation of the cultural dichotomies
are begun will the educated Egyptian feel secure and
survive well in his society.

CHAPTER IX REFERENCES

Benoit, Emile. (1978). "Growth and Defense in
    Developing Countries," Economic Development
    and Cultural Change, 26, 2.
Hussain,Taha. (1984). Preface to Four Soliloquies
    with Allah and the Religious Debate, French
    and Arabic.
Ibrahim, Saad Eddin. (1981). "Superpowers in the
    Arab World," Washington Quarterly, Vol. 4, No.
    3, Summer.

INDEX

Abbas, S., 4, 15, 20
Administration, 128-131, 142,154
Afghani, G., 5
Agarian-Socialism Reform (1952), 41, 43
Al Azhar University, 3, 6, 14, 26, 27, 36
Alexandria (riots), 5, 9
Anglo-Egyptian Treaty (1936), 20
Arab Invasion, 3

Basic Education, 78-30, 99-100, 157
Budget
   (education) 35, 36, 46, 59, 131
Bus Mechanics Training Grant, 98, 101, 111

Cabani, I., 19
Camp David Accords, 54, 103
Canadian International Development and Research
   Center, 89
Catholic Relief Associations, 86
Center for Development of English Language Training,
   93, 101,111, 126, 137, 141-142
Compulsory Schools, 23, 61
Constitution, Egyptian (1922), 23
Copts, 5
   schools, 22
Croomer, Lord (Sir Evelyn Baring), 10, 16, 20, 115

Dunlop, Lord, 19
Domestic Schools, 5

Educational Enrollment, 17, 28, 31-32, 48, 60-61, 87
Egyptian University, 15, 26, 30
Elementary Schools, 23, 24, 31, 33, 36, 42, 81-83
English Language Training, 93, 101, 111, 127, 130,
   137, 139-142
Exams, 84, 86, 141, 152
   British General Certificate Exam, 28
   Thanawaya Ama (Secondary school), 63-64

Facilities, 56, 79-80, 87
Farouk, King, 41
Fatimites., 3
Fouad, Prince, 15
Free Officers, 41, 42
French Law School, 20
Fulbright Grants, 101, 108-110, 141